How to Start and Operate Your Own Design Firm

A Guide
for Interior
Designers and
Architects

ALBERT W.
RUBELING, JR.

Second Edition

ALLWORTH PRESS
NEW YORK

11   10   09   08   07   5   4   3   2   1

Published by Allworth Press
An imprint of Allworth Communications, Inc.
10 East 23rd Street, New York, NY 10010

Cover design by Derek Bacchus
Interior design by Mary Belibasakis
Page composition/typography by Integra Software Services, Pvt., Ltd., Pondicherry, India

ISBN-13: 978-1-58115-474-0
ISBN-10: 1-58115-474-7

Library of Congress Cataloging-in-Publication Data
Rubeling, Albert W.
    How to start and operate your own design firm : a guide for interior designers and architects / Albert W. Rubeling, Jr. — 2nd ed.
        p. cm.
    Includes bibliographical references and index.
    ISBN-13: 978-1-58115-474-0 (pbk.)
    ISBN-10: 1-58115-474-7 (pbk.)
    1. Architectural practice—United States—Management.   2. Architectural services marketing—United States.   I. Title.

    NA1996.R83 2007
    720.68'8—dc22

                                                                        2006100744

To all those designers willing to try

Contents

PART 3: GETTING DOWN TO BUSINESS

Preface

This book is about every designer's dream: starting and operating his or her own design firm.

Few attempt the journey. The tragedy is that many regret on a daily basis not having had the nerve to take the leap. Most do not attempt the journey because of the fear and risk involved. Some have numerous other concerns about the obstacles. Still others do not have a clue about how to start or run a business; all they know is how to design. This book is written to assist the majority of designers to make the decision. There is nothing worse for a person than looking back into the past and having regrets. One of the worst regrets one can have is "I wish I had started my own firm five (or ten, or twenty) years ago, and now it's too late." This is precisely what motivated me in 1981 to start my firm. I saw an opportunity, looked the fear of failure in the eye, and decided, "So what if the new firm fails? There are other firms to work for." I did not want to be bitter for the rest of my life, always wondering "What if. . . ."

This book directly addresses those issues that prevent the majority of designers from creating a practice. It addresses the emotional, as well as the intellectual, challenges designers face once they have made the decision to make the leap and start their firm, with or without a parachute.

Many books are written about the intellectual issues, such as financial, banking, marketing, legal, and insurance considerations, and how to deal with them. And this is important because it is terrible to see so many designers start their firms with no knowledge of business, doomed for failure. It is like seeing lambs led to slaughter. But few books are written about how to handle emotional issues such as fear, risk, guilt, and success—the issues that keep a majority of designers from taking the leap.

This book, in its second edition, has been written based on my twenty-five years of experience starting and building my firm, each and every day. It is my hope that these pages will bring to life the many wonderful experiences as well as the difficult issues one will face, and articulate the actual experience of starting a design firm.

The audience for this book includes students in professional practice courses seeking a perspective on what the business side of design is like, professional interns who are planning their futures, and licensed professionals working for others, but who feel that they can do the job and design it better than can their current place of employment. Further, this book can serve as an organizational tool for those designers who have already started their firms and either can't figure out what is going on or who need a guide to assist them in understanding where they have been and where they plan to go. Finally, it is also written for those who may have lost employment and who feel that they have no other choice, and out of desperation have started a practice.

Starting a new design practice is one of the most exhilarating experiences in one's lifetime. It requires nerve, risk-taking, and above all, self-confidence.

The table of contents is organized in such a way that part 1 will help you make the decision concerning whether to "take the leap" or not. Part 2 discusses the reality of starting the new practice and all the areas of consideration you will have to address. Part 3 will help you organize your thoughts and plans and face those emotional issues that you wake to every day: fear, risk, guilt, success, and the future. Finally, the appendixes of the book include various glossaries for reference when you discuss your new practice with accountants, lawyers, bankers, and insurance brokers.

Each chapter is introduced with quotations from many designers and other notable persons that relate to the topic at hand. These are real-life anecdotes that capture the essence and state of mind of those individuals who have been involved in the struggle. These statements bring to life the real and imagined fear, the hope, the happiness, and the reality of the human spirit in the daily saga of operating a design firm. I felt that adding this personal side would make this book less formal and prescriptive for the reader.

I have also included a list of recommended readings on leadership, passion, entrepreneurship, and growing a successful business. All of these books have had a profound impact on my leadership in guiding my firm's growth and success. They have taught me that as leaders, we are to be passionate in our beliefs and provide purpose, meaning, and candor to all those who we are fortunate enough to meet and touch. They are profound.

It is my hope that you will not only read this entire book to decide if you have what it takes to start a firm, but allow it to be your "silent partner," your comprehensive guide, your reference book to aid you in your journey of success once you have decided to take the leap.

Albert W. Rubeling, Jr., FAIA
July 2006/December 1993

Acknowledgments

As with most authors, I am indebted to many.

The challenge of my life to date has been to maintain the critical balance among family, business career, and my professional activity with the American Institute of Architects. I have been able to maintain this balance (most of the time) because of the care and efforts of the following people:

The employees of Rubeling & Associates, Inc., Architecture + Interior Design, without whose efforts this book could not have been written. They are the individuals responsible for the day-to-day activity, survival, and success of the firm. Most importantly, I need to thank John J. DiMenna, AIA, for his unbelievable loyalty and belief in my vision over the past twenty-four years and for being the analytical, follow-up "doer" that he is. What I start and never finish, he does. Rubeling & Associates, Inc. has been our laboratory along with our other partner, Dave Recchia, AIA, to study various business strategies. Much of the research I have conducted and learned from is the foundation of this book's content.

I am also indebted to Ms. Ann Stacy, Hon. AIA, who, as the executive director of the Baltimore chapter of the American Institute of Architects in 1987–88, gave me the ability to see the overall big-picture benefits of being an active leader in a professional association. Through my travels with the AIA, attendance at conventions, and meeting and conversing with other design professionals, I have come to understand that we all face the same problems in business every day, day in and day out. She has made me believe that I am a leader, and that I need to relay my vision and message to the design community. Because of her belief in me, I have learned that leadership is all about enabling others to act by encouraging their hearts. I have attempted to develop a leadership style that enrolls others in my vision by releasing their brainpower through their need for meaning, direction, hope, and optimism.

Finally, I am indebted to my three sons, Kyle Patrick, Korey Brown, and Kolby Albert. They have been loving, understanding companions on the roller coaster ride of my personal life and architectural practice over the past twenty-five years. I thank them for believing in me and for allowing me to strive for my vision in life. I want to thank my sons for putting up with my leadership activities with numerous community groups and the AIA, since those activities did not always allow me to be home for dinner every night or coach every baseball and lacrosse game when they were young.

My sons have been a constant source of inspiration in my life. My ultimate hope and legacy will be my success in effectively teaching them what lessons I have learned in the first half of my life journey. We have been through some amazing, eventful chapters. I look forward to the second half.

PART 1: Making the Decision

"THE SEARCH FOR THE PERFECT VENTURE CAN TURN INTO PROCRASTINATION.
YOUR IDEA MAY OR MAY NOT HAVE MERIT. THE KEY IS TO GET STARTED."
—Unknown

"NOTHING IS MORE DIFFICULT, AND THEREFORE MORE PRECIOUS,
THAN TO BE ABLE TO DECIDE."
—Napoleon Bonaparte

"IT DOESN'T MATTER WHICH SIDE OF THE FENCE YOU GET OFF
ON SOMETIMES. WHAT MATTERS MOST IS GETTING OFF. YOU CANNOT
MAKE PROGRESS WITHOUT MAKING DECISIONS."
—Jim Rohn

"WHEN YOU CANNOT MAKE UP YOUR MIND WHICH OF TWO EVENLY BALANCED
COURSES OF ACTION YOU SHOULD TAKE—CHOOSE THE BOLDER."
—William Joseph Slim

"WE KNOW WHAT HAPPENS TO PEOPLE WHO STAY IN THE MIDDLE
OF THE ROAD. THEY GET RUN OVER."
—Aneurin Bevan

"WHEN YOU HAVE TO MAKE A CHOICE AND YOU DON'T MAKE IT,
THAT ITSELF IS A CHOICE."
—William James

1
SO YOU WANT TO START
YOUR OWN DESIGN FIRM?

I can remember the first year in business; it was the most romantic time in my design career. My wife was working, we didn't have kids or a mortgage, and all I had to do was worry about myself and my firm. No employees, no payroll. I just lived day to day with my simple practice, having to answer only to my clients and my conscience.

That first year in business was great. It was so simple, I did everything: design, draft, write specifications, write proposals, calculate my time sheet and translate it into an invoice. I typed all the letters and invoices on a typewriter, answered the telephone, balanced the checkbook, set up the accounting system, wrote off my first business expense, and received my first check for payment for architectural services rendered. God, it was great.

I remember answering the telephone for the first time with my new firm's name. Boy, was it awkward. But it was a very proud moment.

CONGRATULATIONS

This is the most exciting time in your design career. For one or more reasons, you know (or think you know) that you want to have your own design firm, with your name on the door—a place where you control the design decisions, where you work with the clients, and where you get the credit, reward, and satisfaction of making it on your own.

As designers, we have all invested many years in our education and in our internship, training to become licensed/certified practitioners. Many of us have spent ten, fifteen, maybe twenty to twenty-five years working in a firm or numerous design firms. We know how to design, we have the knowledge of the building codes, we know how to put a project together. We love our work.

The bottom line questions to be asked, though, are, "Can I be a business person?" "Am I entrepreneurial?" "I am passionate about my design capabilities, but can I be passionate about running a business?" Sadly, most designers are not trained for business. Most college curriculums are silent on the topic, except for maybe one course on "Professional Practice." The common thought in the profession is that we are trained how to think and use our imaginations in college, but we are to learn from others after the academic experience about the reality of design and maybe, just maybe, some business skills.

For most of us, after graduation and experiencing our internships, the business side of the design practice is shielded from our view by the leadership of the firm. It is a mystery. If we progress, and portray the proper organizational qualities expected by the firm, we are promoted to project management and, maybe for the first time, exposed to time management expectations to generate a profit for the firm. Profit—what is that? There is usually a requirement to fill out time sheets to track our efforts on the various projects that we will work on. There is a person in the accounting/business office of the firm who is responsible for collecting, maintaining, and reporting on the status of efforts on a project. Why do they do that?

One of the most difficult transitions for any designer to understand, accept, and practice is the translation of design efforts into a business language that is measurable and meaningful.

As designers, what is our value system? Is it great design? Is it being successful in business?

In my mind, successful designers *must create and maintain a "balance"* in their professional efforts at their design firm. We all know that we can create great design. But can we all be great at business? Understanding that we need to balance our design ego with a time schedule to produce a product in a measurable time frame is the ultimate challenge in creating a successful, profitable design practice.

Is a Design Practice a Business?

A *practice* is the carrying on or exercise of a profession or occupation as a way of life, whereas a *business* is a commercial or mercantile activity customarily engaged in as a means of livelihood. This is a very important issue that you as a designer will struggle with day in and day out for the entire time that you own your firm. Your attitudes on this issue will change daily. For years in design school, we were taught that design is a way of life.

We ate, slept, and drank design. However, when we start a business and amass client responsibilities, accountability, and debt, we quickly become engaged in earning a livelihood. As design firm owners, we are accountable for more than just good design. We are also responsible for deadlines, code issues, public life, welfare, health, and safety, as well as paychecks, benefits, rent, telephone bills, liability insurance, utility bills—the list goes on and on. The challenge of operating a successful design firm is maintaining a balance between design practice and design business principles. There may be times when design concerns must become secondary in order for a business to succeed.

Running a business (design firm) can provide some of the most rewarding accomplishments and some of the most gut-wrenching setbacks that you will ever experience. Business is life! You cannot truly appreciate the good without experiencing and understanding the bad. You will take your business to bed with you every evening, and wake up with it every morning.

Designing a new firm will require many long, hard, devoted hours in the beginning. Like designing a building or a bridge, it requires high creative energy and dedication to purpose. Starting a firm is just the beginning of a journey that will require constant attention to detail, maintenance, and course corrections—until the day you retire, sell, or "close down the shop." Investing time in a future firm's development requires persistence, stamina, and being up for it every morning. Few people possess all these qualities at once. That is why partners were created!

As an individual, you may feel that you are inadequate, that you do not have every trait that it takes to start and operate a design firm. You're not alone. The majority of start-up firms begins with two or more designers as partners, creating the firm because they share a vision and collectively possess the variety of traits necessary to succeed. Many feel the need to share the risk with others. That's okay—it's a natural human trait. In the ideal partnership, each partner complements the other in his or her particular strengths and weaknesses.

Above all, make sure that either you or one of your new partners is entrepreneurial. Using the imagination that you cultivated in design school now, in business, for business purposes, is the key. One of you must look at the new firm as a business and use your imagination to understand that there is more to being successful in this business than being a great designer. You must balance design, production, marketing, administrative needs, human resources, and cash flow to be a success.

CAN YOU BEAT THE ODDS?

Whether you "go it" alone or with a partner, you face extremely challenging odds. Every year, over 1,000 design firms start up in the United States. Of those, 800 survive the first year, 600 get past the second, and only 500 are left at the end of the third. After the end of the fifth year, only 250 of the original 1,000 start-up firms exist in some way or form.

To own and manage your own design firm is one of the greatest and most satisfying challenges you can experience. You'll need sheer determination and an insatiable desire to succeed. Survival depends on success. The toll on personal health and family life can be very dramatic.

Now, considering all of the above, do you have "what it takes" to start your own design firm? How do you prepare for the journey? What are the important considerations to address before making the decision? (If you have made the decision to start, or have already started your firm, you will have already addressed many of the topics about to be discussed. However, let the book help you organize your thoughts and address the issues that you haven't yet dealt with, or even readdress those that you already have encountered.)

One thing that all successful firms share from day one is that their leadership is committed to the success of the business, no matter what. Commitment in time, talent, and resources is key. One must be passionate and committed to the new entity. It is so very difficult to be successful when your mind and heart are only "into" the new venture on a part-time basis. You must be consumed with your efforts.

You must, however, call a time-out on occasion, and be brutally honest with yourself concerning the results of your efforts, to ensure that you are on the path to success. This is the hard part. Pride can get in the way and blind a novice businessperson to challenges, leading to failures. You must measure and maintain balance in your professional, as well as your personal, life to be successful. While you are committed to your business, you must understand that your business is not your life. Many entrepreneurs suffer from being "workaholics." There is more to life than work. In my view, my career—my job—is a means to my end for a "better life." My career has provided a good living, which has allowed me to acquire a residence, educate my children, travel, and partake in numerous life learning experiences that have enriched my family's and friends' time on this earth.

I am proud of being a successful designer, but I am also proud to be a successful parent, teacher, role model, mentor, leader in the community, coach, fan, golfer, and wine advocate.

Founding a firm has led me to help others every day. What matters to me is: COMMITMENT, PASSSION, LEADERSHIP, BALANCE, and HONESTY.

Let's look at what it takes to make the decision to start your firm.

2
FACING THE HARD QUESTIONS

The president of my old firm was my mentor, and he died prematurely of cancer. It was an old-line firm, and the other principals thought I was full of too much piss and vinegar. When my mentor died, every rung in my ladder to the top was neatly sawed to prevent me from obtaining my ambitions to succeed in the firm. I was tired of always having to prove myself to the other principals, and I sure as hell wasn't going to prove myself to principals of another firm. I was running projects and proving myself to the firm's clients, and I felt that I only had to prove myself to me and to clients. That made me decide to leave and start my own firm, and not to work for another firm.

You know, when I used to work for the old firm, there was someone responsible for everything. There was the business manager who was responsible for billing the clients, getting the money in, and handing out the paychecks. The marketing guy sold the firm's experience and brought in the new work. The eldest partner was the patriarch of the firm. His stature as figurehead gave all of us confidence in our abilities to perform. Now I am all alone, and I have to do all of those things. And you know what? It sure is lonely at the top! I can't turn to anyone else but myself for all the decisions. The buck stops all the time with me. On one hand, it is really scary, and on the other, I wouldn't have it any other way because I know that I can handle it, and I know that I will get the job done because I believe in myself.

Making the decision to start your own firm can be one of the easiest or one of the most difficult choices you will make in a lifetime. For some of us, the decision is made by others, or by opportunities that present themselves. For others, it is strictly a personal choice: They simply "jump out of the airplane" and try a start-up, hoping their parachutes will open.

The first question you must ask yourself is: "Why should I start my own firm?"

WHY DO YOU WANT TO START A DESIGN FIRM?

Are you unhappy with your current employer?

Are you dissatisfied with how your current firm practices design?

Do you feel that you can design better than the firm at which you currently work?

Does the leadership of your current employer not respect your skills or opinion on design?

Is having your own firm a lifelong dream?

Do your in-laws need a design for a new vacation home in the islands?

Does your brother-in-law need a design for his new restaurant?

Have any of the firm's clients whom you have worked with as a project designer approached you for their next deal?

Can you and your studio colleague set the world on fire and show those stodgy principals in your firm who is better?

Are you, heaven forbid, driven by money, and convinced that you can make more by having your own firm than by working for others?

Are you tired of having to prove yourself to the unappreciative principals in your current firm?

Did you attempt to start a firm in the past and fail to get off the ground?

If so, did you learn a great deal from your experience, and now you want to try again?

You need to come to terms with yourself as soon as possible on these issues. Accept the answers and use them as a "driving force" on your journey to success. Making the decision to start a firm is very serious, but it is not life threatening! Once you have committed yourself, you can be certain that the road ahead will be long, winding, tumultuous on occasion, and blocked by obstacles. If your new firm fails (and that could happen), it not only may wreak havoc with your personal savings and other assets, but also may deal a blow to your ego.

However, failing at a start-up is not the end of the world. You can always get another job with another design firm or, heaven forbid, have a change in career. Stop and ponder what the worst thing is that could happen. Develop plans A, B, and C, just in case.

As stated in the first chapter, many designers fail in their first start-ups, but the important issue is to learn from the experience. Founding a design firm is not for everyone, thank heavens. If so, there would be millions of sole proprietors, and who would get the large design projects? In this life there are followers and there are leaders. You need to decide which one you are.

Working for someone else offers many advantages:

You have regular hours, with occasional overtime to meet an
   important deadline.
Your evenings and weekends can remain free for family, friends,
   and hobbies.
You can expect to receive occasional pay increases over the years.
Your personal savings and assets are not at risk in the business.
The worst thing that can happen to you is that if you "screw up"
   significantly on a project you can lose your job. You will not be
   sued or have liability for your negligent efforts.

You also need to weigh the drawbacks of running a business:

You will need to perform tasks and chores that you used to delegate
   and that you dislike or actually abhor.
You will not escape being "boss free." Your clients and suppliers will
   become your new bosses.
Your new firm will consume just about all your time and energy.
You will have little time to spare for family, friends, or hobbies.
You will be responsible and liable for all of your actions. You can't
   fire yourself. You can't hide. The "buck stops with you."

Now ask yourself the crucial question: "What characteristics do I need to make it on my own?"

ENTREPRENEURS

First, and foremost, you or your partner should be an entrepreneur or have the entrepreneurial spirit. What is an entrepreneur? An entrepreneur is a person who organizes and manages any enterprise, especially a business, usually with considerable initiative and risk.

Some of the reasons that entrepreneur designers start their own firms are:

Independence: a strong desire to be their own boss
A desire for recognition, prestige, and fame
An opportunity to earn far more than they could working for others
The discovery of an opportunity that others have missed or ignored
The challenge to compete against their former employer

Starting a firm will have a major impact on one's spouse and family or significant other. Being married to an entrepreneur is difficult, especially if both marital partners do not share the same instincts. It is hard for a spouse to understand what motivates a designer to start his or her own firm. How can someone give up job security and take on what appears to be unacceptable risks? What will the spouse get in return? Long hours and dedicated hard work, with no guarantees. It borders on the irrational!

CHART 1
Personal Qualities of an Entrepreneur

Adaptable	Imaginative
Bold	Impassioned
Confident	Independent
Considerate of others	Innovative
Diplomatic	Inquisitive
Disciplined	Motivated
Driven	Passionate
Energetic	Self-controlled
Ethical	Sociable
Flexible	Tactful
Healthy	Timely

Nevertheless, if the entrepreneurial spirit is incredibly strong in someone, it is very difficult to talk it out of him or her. The motivations are complex and differ from one person to another. In addition to drive, willingness to take chances, and persistence, the personal qualities shown in chart 1 characterize an entrepreneur.

The entrepreneur *is* the business (firm) and is usually its founder, its motivation, and its force. Do you have any of the qualities outlined in the chart? They are some entrepreneurial characteristics that drive designers to start and operate their own firms.

You don't need to possess all of these traits to be an entrepreneur, but don't kid yourself; if you don't possess many of them and still decide to open your own business, you will be in for one of the shocks of your life—failure.

CHART 2
Questions to Answer to Help You Make the Decision

What do I want out of life?

What are my aspirations, and are they attainable?

Am I prepared to work hard and make sacrifices?

What am I passionate about? Design? Money? Success? Family?

What are my core values?

Do I care for others? Do I want to help others succeed?

Am I a self-starter?

Can I finish what I start?

Do I have common sense?

Am I in good health?

Do I have enough professional design and/or business experience?

Am I an entrepreneur? Manager? Or producer? Can I do them all?

Can I lead others?

Can I delegate work and responsibilities?

Can I take responsibility?

Am I a good organizer?

Am I a procrastinator?

Can I make decisions?

Do people trust what I say?

Do I have a vision?

Am I a "driver," or do I need a partner who is?

What kind of manager am I?

Can I be honest with myself?

What are my strengths and weaknesses? How do I address and supplement them to be well-rounded?

Can I afford to start my own firm? What are my life responsibilities?

"Successful" entrepreneurs are willing to work hard. They get along well with others. They have good communications skills. They know how to organize. They take pride in all that they do. They are self-starters. They welcome responsibility and are willing and able to make decisions.

So before you commit yourself to an extraordinary investment of time, energy, ego, and money, think about and answer the questions posed in chart 2 above.

This short personal appraisal is by no means an evaluation of whether or not you are a qualified entrepreneur. It is simply a means of focusing on your personal attributes and will help you decide on taking that major step. However, you may want to ask your close friends and/or colleagues to evaluate you so that you can get a more objective review. A word of warning: Do not ask your spouse or significant other to evaluate you. He or she will be more emotional than intellectual, and will give a highly subjective review.

If you can be brutally honest with yourself and you come up short in some areas, an option that you have is to consider having a partner to address those areas of need that you do not possess.

WHY DO DESIGNERS WANT TO START A FIRM WITH A PARTNER?

Many designers feel the need to share the day-to-day issues in starting and operating their new firm. Either they do not feel qualified to do it alone or they cannot bear the thought of assuming all the risk themselves. Others are presented opportunities, such as these:

My studio colleague and I were laid off on the same day. We've both been moonlighting on residential projects, so we decided to help each other out and form a trial partnership over the next two months. What do we have to lose?

My colleague, who left his firm a year ago, just landed a large project and wants me to leave my secure position and help him out. He wants me to join him now, and become a partner in a few months.

Do you recall the question in chapter 1 under "So You Want to Start Your Own Design Firm?" You need to ask those very questions of your potential partner. Developing a partnership with another is very similar to marriage. It requires an understanding of each other and the development of a commitment, in sickness and in health, for richer or for poorer. Does this sound familiar? Partners are business spouses. Many marriages end in divorce, as do partnerships. Be careful. This is serious business, and you should level with your partner on all the issues. Use the Partner Sanity Tests (charts 3 and 4) in this chapter to serve as a beginning point in your discussions with your partner(s). Have fun with this exercise! Have both or all of you considering partnership fill out the charts. Then sit down and take the time to discuss the results.

CHART 3
Partner Sanity Test 1: Awareness

Vision and Goals

What vision do I have for the future company?

What goals do I have as a designer?

What goals do I have as a businessperson?

Do my partners share my vision and goals?

What if they don't?

What are my expectations of the new company?

What are my expectations of myself?

What are my expectations of my partner(s)?

Am I an entrepreneur? How about my partner(s)?

Administration

What is business administration?

Do I understand the business administration needs for the new firm?

Am I interested in doing some or all of the administration?

Do I expect my partners to do it?

Am I weak in business administration because I have never been exposed to it?

If all of us are weak in this area, to whom can we talk?

Do I have a mentor whom I can speak with on this topic?

When should we hire staff?

Finance

Do I understand the financial requirements of a business?

Do my partners?

Should we each put money up front in the firm? How much?

Do I understand how to spend money wisely?

Should I handle the checkbook and other records?

Do I expect my partners to handle the records?

Do I understand the importance of cash in a business?

Am I willing to be the financial person, paying the bills and calling all the clients to collect our money?

Do I expect my partners to do that?

Do I know how to establish fees? Hourly rates?

Do I understand overhead? Do my partners?

Do I want to deal with the accountant and the IRS? Do my partners?

Do I want to deal with bankers?

Do I understand financial statements? Income and profit and loss statements?

Do my partners?

Marketing

What is marketing? Will I be doing it, or my partner(s), or both?

What image do we want the firm to have?

What will the new firm's name be?

How are we going to market the firm?

In what niche markets are we strong?

What will be our service offerings?

Do I know how to write a proposal? Do my partners?

Do I know how to sell to clients? Do my partners?

Legal

Do I understand the legal considerations that face a new business? Do my partners?

Will I or we select the lawyer?

With what form of business am I comfortable? My partner(s)?

Do I understand design and construction contracts? Will I write them or will my partner(s)?

Insurance

Do I understand what insurance is for?

How much insurance is enough?

Should I get Professional Liability Insurance or "go naked" for a time? Do I care?

Do I like dealing with insurance issues? Salespeople?

Will my partner(s) deal with insurance?

Office and Equipment

Where will our new firm be located? In my house or a partner's house? Downtown or in the suburbs?

Do I understand commercial leases? Do my partners?

Do I understand the technology that I need versus want?

Will I be doing the work? Will my partners?

Should I purchase an expensive plotter, or subcontract out printing to a vendor or another design firm that has a plotter?

Design (The Land Mine!)

Will I be the firm's designer? Will my partner(s)?

Can we share design responsibilities and philosophy?

Who will control the design philosophy?

What are our design goals as a firm?

Production / Bidding / Construction

Do I know how to do working drawings?

Do my partners?

Do I know how to write specifications? Do my partners?

Do I want to do production work or only design?

Do I understand building and fire codes? Do my partners understand these codes?

Do I know how to bid a project and issue addenda?

Can I conduct a bid opening?

What are my expectations? What do I expect of my partner(s)?

Will I do shop drawings? Will my partner(s)?

Will I handle construction administration on-site and in the office? Will my partner(s)?

You will be amazed at how effective this exercise will be in flushing out any concerns and issues that the new entity will face in-house. Be responsible! The discussion could last for hours or maybe a few days. But consider how important a first step it is in obtaining a successful journey. (If you have already formed a partnership and are in practice, don't ignore this exercise. You can still benefit from its focus on awareness and personal strengths.)

WEIGHING THE ADVANTAGES AND DRAWBACKS OF A PARTNERSHIP

Chart 3 above, on awareness, will help you and your partner(s) document your expectations of yourself and of each other. After you discuss the results and learn more about yourselves, go on to chart 4 to evaluate your strengths and weaknesses in the seven key categories listed. Compare your results with those of your partner(s). The results should pinpoint all the advantages and drawbacks you feel about having this/these partner(s). The results should also identify those problematic areas in which none of you has expertise, and which you may have to address or become knowledgeable about. This test should have an incredible emotional impact on you and your partner(s), helping you search out any hidden agendas or uncommunicated expectations. Consider having a good friend, colleague, or business advisor sit in on the discussion so that you can have another intellectual perspective on your outcome.

WHAT CHARACTERISTICS SHOULD MY PARTNER(S) HAVE SO THAT WE WILL MAKE IT ON OUR OWN?

By going through the exercises in charts 3 and 4, you and your partner(s) will have a written and oral record of the major topics that affect a business, including a partnership.

Believe it or not, most partnerships do not conduct any exercises like these. The partners assume, presume, or expect whatever they choose of their partner(s). Most designers do not want to take the time to effectively communicate their thoughts, expectations, and aspirations on business topics because they either are not organized or do not feel knowledgeable enough on the subjects. They just want to design and leave all those other tasks as "necessary evils" for a partner to deal with.

CHART 4
Partner Sanity Test 2: Strengths and Weaknesses

Evaluate your strengths and weaknesses in the following categories:

	Strengths	*Weaknesses*
Administration		
Finance		
Marketing		
Legal		
Insurance		
Design		
Production/ Bidding/ Construction		

The major factor facing partners in a design firm is ego. Designers may or may not be strong in business affairs, but most are confident that they are good or the best when it comes to design. This trait can wreak serious havoc in a partnership. Many attempt to temper the issue by making each partner responsible for his or her own client's design work, and then sharing responsibilities for the remaining day-to-day requirements of the firm. Others couldn't possibly operate that way! Talk it over with your potential partner(s).

If you take the time to go through the Partner Sanity Test, you will be light years ahead of the majority of partnerships in practice. It may be difficult to take the time and expose your raw feelings and nerves to your potential (or real) partner(s), but isn't it worth the few extra days? Half the battle is organizing the topics. The Partner Sanity Test does this for you. The rest is up to you.

Obviously, once you have completed the exercises, all the bases of practice should be covered. If not, at least they will be identified, and you and your partner(s) can discuss who can best handle them, either individually or jointly. Use the test results to discuss and assign who will be responsible for each activity, according to your documented strengths and weaknesses. In a successful partnership, each member's strengths and weaknesses complement the other's.

Also, as stated before, entrepreneurial vision is needed to lead the new firm. If neither one (or none) of you is an entrepreneur, you need to seriously consider the relationship. Is it possible for one of you to develop entrepreneurial skills? What if both (or all) of you are entrepreneurs? It will take effort to make sure that you stay out of each other's way. Is there enough room in one firm for so many chiefs? Talk it out. You will be much better off if you do so now rather than later—when the partnership fails and good people are trying to figure out what went wrong, and a lot of money is being spent on lawyers and attorneys.

Finally, these are the ultimate questions to ask about each of your potential partners:

Do I want to jump out of the plane with this person as my partner?
What happens if my partner's chute doesn't open? Will I help?
If my chute doesn't open, will my partner help?
Will my partner be around in good times and in bad, in sickness and in health, for richer or for poorer?

DO I FISH, OR CUT BAIT?

Once you have answered all the questions above truthfully to yourself and your partner(s), and you are confident that you and your partner(s) have what it takes to start a successful design firm, do it! Remember the saying "Nothing ventured, nothing gained." Be true to yourself. If you feel that you have what it takes to start a firm, and you let small worries get in your way, you may regret your indecision for the rest of your life.

How many unhappy friends and colleagues do you know who didn't take the registration exam or start their own firms because of fear, and ended up bitter and jealous of others who did attempt to succeed? Will you be able to live with yourself in the future if you're always wondering "what if"? There will always be an excuse to not "jump out of the plane." Timing, your health, your family, your spouse, your mortgage, the money—the list can go on and on and on, for as long as you want it to. Few attempt to bypass the excuses and take the leap. Once you have made the decision, you need to focus on the start-up issues that lie ahead of you, out there, as you begin your new firm.

Finally, be honest with yourself and install a "governor," or conscience, on your new enterprise. Establish some first year goals to achieve. Constantly measure them: daily, weekly, and monthly. You may achieve your design goals, but if you do not accomplish your financial goals, you need to be honest and rethink your start-up decision. If you do not achieve your marketing goals, you need to reevaluate your decision. You must have a plan B and plan C in mind, should your start-up not achieve your targets. Too many designers hang onto *hope*, and are blinded by the euphoric experience of their firm start-ups to the point that they ignore their business needs and fail financially.

As long as you remain true to yourself and strive for, measure, and achieve your interim goals, you will succeed.

PART 2: The Reality of a Start

"THE SECRET OF GETTING AHEAD IS GETTING STARTED. THE SECRET
OF GETTING STARTED IS BREAKING YOUR COMPLEX OVERWHELMING
TASKS INTO SMALL MANAGEABLE TASKS, AND THEN STARTING
ON THE FIRST ONE."
—Mark Twain

"THE STARTING POINT OF ALL ACHIEVEMENT IS DESIRE."
—Napoleon Hill

"THERE ARE TWO MISTAKES ONE CAN MAKE ALONG THE ROAD
TO TRUTH . . . NOT GOING ALL THE WAY, AND NOT STARTING."
—Buddha

3
INVESTING IN YOURSELF

"Control your destiny or someone else will!"
—JACK WELCH

"The best you can do for someone else is to be yourself."
—AARON EISENBERGER

The buck stops here! I am responsible for everything that this firm produces. I design, I draft, I specify, I build models, I invoice, I write the proposal, I write contracts, I buy insurance, I answer the telephone, I work on the computer, I work late at night, I visit the job site, I program, I space-plan, I check requisitions, I check shop drawings, I market, I do everything! Since I do all these things, I must remember to wear the different hat that comes with each job. I can't charge the client the same hourly rate for drafting a detail as I do for designing or writing a specification section—that wouldn't be fair. One minute I can charge $95 per hour, and the next $25 per hour! How am I going to keep it all straight?

If I am going to be working sixteen hours a day, and I have enough work to keep myself busy, when do I market for the next job? How can I do two things at once—draw at my desk and market? What is marketing anyway? How can I promote myself if I am at the office all day, or on a job site, or traveling all day? Where is the next project coming from?

I learned to type in high school. I can type about forty-five words a minute. But you know, I can type only so many letters and invoices and spec sections. I am an architect, but when I started my own firm, I didn't have any money to pay for a secretary. My answering machine did a great job handling the phone, but having to type all the specs for a project cut into the time available for my work. What I did was to hire one of the secretaries from the old firm on a part-time basis in the evening and on weekends. She typed all my specs and agreed to get paid when I got paid. She did a great job, and we continued doing business that way for the next year!

You invested thousands of dollars and hours of blood, sweat, and tears in your design training and education. Countless hours were spent in the design studio as you unwound endless rolls of bumwad in search of the greatest design solutions. Thousands more were devoted to studying the works of the masters, learning form, function, and style. That is the role of the design academic institution.

But how much time did you spend learning about how a design firm operates? A design firm is a business. Most of us could not have cared less in our professional practice classes during the last semester of design school. We felt that we learned design and history in five or six years, and would have the rest of our lives to deal with contracts, administration, finances, and marketing. In fact, that was a job for the principals in the firms that we would work for. We just wanted to get a job, hold onto it, get as much experience as possible to sit for the registration exam, and finally become licensed to practice.

Dealing with all these start-up issues sounds scary, doesn't it? When you think about it, however, running a business is similar to living life day to day. You learn something every day, and you must build upon it to gain more knowledge, wisdom, and experience. Some people find living life scary, and if you are one of them, do yourself a favor and don't start your own firm.

The reality of a start-up, as any designer who has founded his or her own firm will tell you, is that it takes a lot more nerve than brains. That's the truth. Jumping out of the airplane is only half the battle! The other half is mastering the air currents, landing safely, and getting up on your feet.

It is humanly impossible to deal with all the start-up issues at one time or in a limited time span. Come to think of it, many designers who have had their firms for over ten years still haven't dealt with all the start-up issues! So how do you handle something that appears so formidable—starting a firm, dealing with the issues, and coping with success?

. . . .
The secret to starting a firm and addressing the issues is to recognize the fact that a business is a **journey**, *not a destination.*
. . . .

If you think about it, you will realize that you can't brush your teeth in the morning unless you wake up first. You can't drink a cup of coffee until you either make or buy a cup. The reality of a start-up is that there are many issues to address, and you must deal with them one at a time—at the appropriate time—as you grow into the business. Let success and growth help you through all the start-up issues. Be logical and let the business expand through a natural progression.

For example, if you are starting your firm alone, you certainly do not need to have a phone system with thirty-two lines, or a retirement plan designed for fifteen employees, or a network of ten personal computers (PCs). Nor do you need an expensive new company car or an office located on the top floor of the tallest building in town. Be sensible! Purchase what you absolutely need to get the job done, and that's it.

Remember, a start-up business is a major investment of time and money. One of the toughest issues to deal with is money, or the lack of it. When you start a firm, one thing is for sure: More money goes out than comes in! Just think about all the equipment and accessories that your former employer had. You will need to purchase much of the same over a period of time.

Forget a salary for a while! The only way to develop success in a young start-up company is to constantly reinvest time, money, and profits. Just take home enough money to live on. Invest the rest into the firm, because it will be the best investment of your life. This is the single most important unwritten rule shared by all true entrepreneurs.

. . . .
If you invest your money in stocks or businesses other than your own, you have more confidence in those businesses than in your own.
. . . .

Confidence says a lot about yourself and your abilities. True entrepreneurs feel that no one can achieve success better than they can in their own business.

THE JOURNEY BEGINS

The reality of starting your own firm is being ready for the roller coaster ride of your life. This is one of the most dynamic life decisions you can make. The novelty of having your name on that "shingle" is short-lived and only skin deep. The journey that you will take can be the most exasperating as well as exciting adventure imaginable. Your firm will become a way of life for you.

Remember balance.

We turn next to the major considerations that you have to face in starting your new enterprise.

4
VISION AND GOAL SETTING

"All our dreams can come true, if we have the courage to pursue them."

—WALT DISNEY

"Be the change you want to see in the world."

—MAHATMA GANDHI

My goal in the first year of business was to gross what my salary was at the old firm, which was $16,000. Well, when I did that in six months, I thought it was an aberration! At the end of the year, the company grossed $32,000—more than double!

Most people who never started their own business think that it is all easy, and that you can take time off at will, go places, and do as you please. The truth of the matter is that it is easy to enslave yourself to your firm. If you have any kind of work ethic, your conscience will take over, and you will feel guilty when you are not working. Be fair to yourself and don't worry about how others view you.

VISION

What is vision in life or business? Vision is a trait of an individual or group of people who have the ability to anticipate what will or may come to pass. Some refer to visionaries as dreamers, because they look to the future. A more appropriate word for vision is imagination. All of us have imagination.

As designers, we were trained in design school or by our mentors to expand our minds to think about objects in three dimensions.

Having vision is one of the most powerful traits one can possess in business. Being able to imagine the future and develop a plan to obtain one's goals successfully is a powerful ability. As designers, we all can imagine the conceptual final product before we refine the design over and over again. Often, the final design may be a little different than the one that we originally imagined. However, usually it is 90 percent of our original thought.

Most designers have this inherent design vision. Many, however, cannot apply the same principles and techniques to business. For example, when one architect was asked "Where do you expect to be in five years with your practice?" the response was "I don't know, I can't even predict tomorrow! I guess I'll know in five years!" Another architect, who is a bit more visionary, responded "I hope to still be in business with a staff of ten, providing design services in the restaurant market niche and the hotel market niche. The firm will be located in the city in approximately 3,000 square feet of office space, and I'll probably have another partner by then."

What is the difference between the two statements? The fact of the matter is that both have some factual basis. However, the first, while being apparently true, is very short-sighted and doesn't take into account possible opportunities and hope. The second statement, whether partially obtainable or totally wrong, establishes hopes for the individual or firm to strive for and obtain.

Vision is 20/20 only in hindsight! Looking ahead and predicting the future is difficult and challenging. But trying to imagine the rewards and obstacles you will encounter in the future is a fun part of the business game.

As designers, we are trained to "turn a client's vision into a reality." What you need to do as a businessperson is to harness your design vision abilities and focus them on business activity. You have the ability, the imagination. *So use it!*

What vision(s) do you think that you have? How about your partner(s)? Examine your vision(s). It is important that you or at least one partner has the ability to exercise business imagination. The fact of the matter is that vision, drive, and imagination are your road map to and through the future. Otherwise, you would wander aimlessly through each day. Imagination and vision set the course.

One of the many gifts designers have is an imagination that is more highly developed than that of the average person. We exercise our imaginations every day. Apply this power to your thoughts on your business. You will be amazed with yourself.

Take your dreams and visions, utilize your imagination, and develop strategies to obtain the goals, both personal and business, that you want out of life.

GOAL SETTING

It is important in life as well as business to set goals. Goals are basically targets to aim for in the journey to success. Every businessperson wants to be successful, but since each of us is different, we may set different goals to achieve our success.

It is just as easy to set good goals as bad ones. Good goals should be set not only for business but for personal and family matters as well. Here are some examples of good, personal goals:

Exercise every day.
Stop smoking cigarettes.
Stay healthy.
Provide the best education for the kids.
Take a great family vacation.
Plan an anniversary getaway to somewhere exotic.
Eat breakfast every day.
Have dinner with the family five out of seven evenings.
Obtain a balance among business, family, and personal needs.
Play golf or some other sport at least three times per month to
    help deal with stress.
Get to bed early every evening.
Arise at the same time every day.
Develop good work habits.
Address all those I encounter—friends, family, and clients—as if they
    had signs around their necks saying, "Make me feel important!"

Bad goals essentially are targets established in a vacuum. Such goals lack focus and vision because the path to obtain them is not clear or well defined.

An unfocused goal is not only difficult to obtain but also frustrating to attempt. Many designers establish vague goals in their careers, such as:

"My goal is to have my own practice, someday."

"I want to produce the most creative architecture in the area!"

"Maybe I'll work for this firm for another year. After that I don't know. I'll work for another firm that will challenge me more and appreciate my design talent."

"I'll wait until the right opportunity hits, and bang, I'm out of this firm on my own!"

GOALS FOR YOUR DAILY ROUTINE—AND BEYOND

If you want to be successful in life and obtain happiness, you must learn to establish realistic, obtainable goals on a daily basis, with an overview of long-range goals that serve as your "vision" about yourself.

In your daily routine, it is important to establish small, obtainable goals, sometimes referred to as "inchpebbles." Simple goals, to be obtained on a daily basis, may include not only waking up at 6:00 A.M. but getting out of bed at 6:00 A.M.! Simple goals in business may include starting your day consistently at 8:00 A.M., making two marketing cold calls per day, designing your projects in the morning when you are rested and fresh, and conducting administrative and marketing functions in the afternoon, when most of your clients are out of meetings and in their offices, available for communication. Long-range goals—"milestones"—in the journey of success—are visionary and need to be the sum of many inchpebbles.

Remember, the definition of a work goal is an end that you strive to obtain. If you are the type of person who needs structure in your daily routine, you should read the many paperbacks on "minute manager" techniques. Challenge yourself! Set goals, both milestones and inchpebbles, and you will be amazed at how quickly you begin to work in an organized fashion, contain fear and risk, and start to realize your dreams!

Sample Daily Goals
Awake at 6:00 A.M.
Eat breakfast every day.
Arrive at the office at 8:00 A.M.

Manage time effectively: design in the morning, take lunch at noon, handle marketing and client contacts in the afternoon, and "administrate" in the evening.

Be billable (chargeable) to clients for six to eight hours per day.

Market at least one hour per day on average.

"Administrate" for the firm at least two hours per day on average.

Record daily activities accurately through a time management system.

Generate an average of $500 or $_____ per day in cash flow for the firm to operate.

Reflect at the end of the day: "What did I accomplish today? How does it relate to my overall goals?"

Weekly Goal Evaluation

Did I accomplish five marketing cold calls this week?

Did I put in the production time that I needed to make the deadlines?

Was I billable forty hours this week? If not, why not? Next week?

Did I generate $2,500 or $_____ this week in cash flow for operations?

Have I kept aware of trends and competitive forces and their impact on the firm?

Sample Monthly Goals

Twenty marketing cold calls per month

Thirty new marketing leads per month

An average of 160 hours of billable time per month

Forty hours of administration time per month on average

$_____ invoicing per month

$_____ expenses per month

$_____ profit per month

Sample Annual Goals

Two hundred marketing cold calls per year

Three hundred new marketing leads per year

Two thousand hours of billable time per year

Four hundred hours of administration time per year

$_____invoicing per year

$_____expenses per year

$_____profit per year

MONITORING EFFORTS AND RESULTS

An important part of setting goals and working to achieve them is monitoring your efforts in the process. With many goals, there will be a major difference between the effort exerted and the results achieved. Some goals are relatively simple to state but difficult to obtain. Conversely, others are simple to achieve but difficult to recognize. Be patient. Achieving daily goals is what the journey to success is all about. It will be frustrating at times, but the pursuit of your dreams will make life for you, your family, and your new business highly rewarding.

Remember to measure your results, not your effort. Keep score of the game in points, not in how many shots you take!

Goal setting is an ongoing exercise. As with the design process, you need to set the easy, obtainable goals first to gain confidence and develop momentum. This will help you gain the confidence you need to tackle the more difficult, complex goals of life—whether they involve business, personal, or family issues.

Challenge yourself! Use your imagination. Set goals—both milestones and inchpebbles—toward your vision in business. Be careful. Don't set vague goals or too many goals. Record them in your mind and write them down. (Business and marketing plans are discussed in later chapters.) You are on your way to realizing your dreams!

5

FINANCIAL CONSIDERATIONS

"The surest way to ruin a man who does not know how to handle money is to give him some."
—GEORGE BERNARD SHAW

"Sometimes your best investments are the ones you don't make."
—DONALD TRUMP

"Where large sums of money are concerned, it is advisable to trust nobody."
—AGATHA CHRISTIE

"The most important thing for a young man is to establish a credit.. a reputation, character."
—JOHN D. ROCKEFELLER

"The hardest thing to understand in the world is the income tax."
—ALBERT EINSTEIN

My first year in business, I refused to have debt. I paid cash for everything! Boy, have times changed.

Having to retain the services of an accountant is scary. First of all, I truly do not understand what accountants do, and I do not know how to read financial statements. I know that I need an accountant because I do not know how or when to file my income taxes for my company. I hope that I will select the right accountant.

I don't invest in the stock market or in any other company but my own. I feel that if I did so, it would mean that I thought other companies were a better investment, that I didn't totally believe in myself or my company. I invest my profits and dollars back into my company and myself because they are the best investment that I can control.

Now that you are a bona fide candidate to start your own firm, you must face the primary issue that all business founders must deal with: money. "How much do I need to start? How much is it going to cost me to operate? Can I afford to start my own firm?"

As much as we all agree as designers that design and being of service are important, the lifeblood of the firm is money. Like it or not, we all need money to live. Some of us need more than others, but money is the way to measure success and to keep score in business. Baseball teams measure success in runs, football and basketball teams in points, businesses in dollars.

WHAT ARE YOUR FINANCIAL NEEDS?

The first question that you must answer is how much money you need to live on each and every *month*, not how much money do you need to get through a given year. Does your spouse have an income? How much money do you spend each week? Don't just think, "I need a salary of $45,000 per year to live." If you do not know how much money you need, sit down and analyze your expenses and spending habits over the last year, or review what happened to last month's paycheck(s). You will be surprised by how you spend money. This primary step is crucial to help you diminish your business risk. However, it is important to understand that what you think your needs are and what they really are may be different. Be honest with yourself, because if you do not produce the income that you *need* from your new business startup, you have to reevaluate what your personal life expenses are. What expenses could be cut if you produce less income? Do your kids go to private or public school? What about a new car versus keeping the old one? You are totally responsible for developing and maintaining the balance of what you make in income and how you spend it. To be successful, you must live within your means.

HOW MUCH MONEY DO YOU NEED TO INVEST TO GET STARTED?

Starting a business requires sacrifices. You will be amazed at how successful you can be with little or no money if you plan your start-up correctly.

You need to approach your new venture with lots of careful thinking and sound planning if you want to succeed. Your capital requirements should be diligently formulated well in advance of taking the plunge. Chart 5 should help you figure out what your personal financial needs are, while chart 6 will help you determine which start-up costs will be necessary for your business.

CHART 5
Financial Needs Checklist

Month of _____

Item	Actual	Proposed budget	Deviation
HOUSING			
Monthly payment			
Taxes			
Insurance			
UTILITIES			
Water			
Cable			
Telephone			
Cell phone			
Heat/air conditioning			
Electricity			
Internet			
CLOTHING			
Yours			
Your spouse's			
The kids'			
FOOD			
Eating out			
Eating in			

(Continued)

Item	Actual	Proposed budget	Deviation
AUTOMOBILE			
Payment			
Gasoline			
Maintenance			
Insurance			
CREDIT			
Credit cards			
Installment loans			
Student loans			
OTHER			
Life insurance			
Education (family)			
Medical and dental			
Taxes			
Recreation			
Travel			
Donations (church/charity)			
Miscellaneous			
INVESTMENTS/ SAVINGS			
Total			

Why do some designers start with $2,000, others with $10,000, and still others with $100,000? The answer lies in the direction, image, and amount of work that a new founder has and wants to develop.

You need initial capital to cover many of your start-up costs. After you decide what advice you need, what equipment to purchase, and where you are going to practice, you can strategize and spend your initial investment dollars wisely. Why hire the largest law firm in the area to set up your organization if you have a friend or close associate who will do it for a very reasonable fee? Do you have to have an office in the high-rent district? Maybe working out of your home is right for you and your new firm. Will inexpensive business cards do the trick in the beginning rather than overwhelmingly expensive ones? Only you can answer these questions. The point here is to think before you act to spend that precious commodity of cash in the beginning. Think this through very clearly and carefully. One of the most common causes of start-up failure is lack of capital. Chart 6 will help you identify some of the start-up expenses associated with a new design firm.

CHART 6
Start-Up Costs Checklist

Expense	Estimated cost	Actual cost	Date to pay
BUSINESS LICENSE/PERMIT(S)			
PROFESSIONAL LICENSE(S)			
BUSINESS OPENING ANNOUNCEMENT			
RENTAL DEPOSIT (if not in home, two months' rent)			
TELEPHONE INSTALLATION (if not in home)			
ANSWERING SERVICE			
UTILITY DEPOSITS (if not in home)			
INSURANCE			
Health			
General liability			
Professional liability			
Life			
Theft			
Disability			
LEGAL			
Initial consultation			
Form of business papers			
ACCOUNTING			
Initial consultation			
Format resolution			

(Continued)

Expense	Estimated cost	Actual cost	Date to pay
PROFESSIONAL ASSOCIATION DUES			
Local			
State			
National			
INITIAL BUSINESS "BROCHURE"			
LETTERHEAD/ BUSINESS CARDS			
EQUIPMENT/ FURNITURE			
Computer hardware			
Computer software			
CADD Plotter			
Copier desk(s)			
Lamps			
File cabinet(s)			
Flat file(s)			
Conference table			
Chair(s)			
Telephone and/ or cell phone			
Telephone answering machine/voice mail			
Facsimile machine			
Photocopying machine			
Coffee maker			
Library shelving			
SUPPLIES			
Pens/pencils			
Markers			
Bumwad/tracing paper			
Paper clips			
Post-it notes			
Legal pads			
Computer disks			

Expense	Estimated cost	Actual cost	Date to pay
Light bulbs			
Measuring tapes			
Digital camera			
Photocopy paper			
MISCELLANEOUS			
Total			

SOURCES OF CAPITAL

Where does start-up capital come from? All knowledgeable business consultants recommend that at least half, if not all, of your initial business investment should come from your own personal reserves. You may have to work for a while at that job that you do not like, but the fact is that if you invest your own dollars on the venture, you send a signal to bankers, accountants, lawyers, and clients that you believe in what you're doing. If you own your home or other real estate, there is the possibility of a home equity loan. Another source of capital may be the cash value amassed in a life insurance policy over the years. Some designers approach friends and/or family for the initial investment. Only you know how real and practical this approach is. If you do borrow money from friends or family members, you should work out a payment schedule. Be prepared. They will have difficulty restraining themselves from getting involved in the operation of your firm. Banks will lend money to start-up firms on rare occasions. Most often, a bank is interested in offering funds for operating capital to businesses that have a track record. For your purposes, the bank's primary value will be for short-term loans for purchases of equipment and other assets. Remember, the amount of initial capital needed to start a design firm is not substantial. Think, and spend wisely.

LEARN HOW TO SPEND MONEY

As stated earlier in this book, one of the most important goals in operating a business is to have more money coming in than going out. Controlling the cash flow of the business is part of controlling overhead. Be very frugal in spending those earned dollars. Ask yourself if spending money on this purchase is for a "necessity" or a "luxury." Another question to ask is "will this purchase make me more effective in my business? Will it save me time?" Be honest with yourself concerning all expenditures. Don't just buy something because others have done it. Think about how it will help you be more efficient and make more profit. Make this process a "conscience" in spending money.

If the proposed expenditure is a necessity and it will also favorably impact your business, then go ahead and spend the funds. However, remember it is easy to justify emotional needs for ego purposes. Intellectually, sometimes it is better to say no to that expensive letterhead or that high-priced rent. When you spend money for the company's benefit, think of it as spending money not for "you" but for someone else, maybe that "other you." Think twice.

Having a partner or a mentor can be good and bad when it comes to making decisions to spend those precious dollars. A partner can be a valuable check-and-balance system. But serious conflicts can arise if you cannot agree on how, when, in what quantities, or why your new company should spend money.

The easiest way to control the expenditure of money is to develop a preliminary operating budget. Budgeting will be easy at first since your new firm will have relatively little overhead or accounts receivable. Just remember the golden rule: "Don't spend more than comes in."

The basic purpose of a preliminary budget is to identify your income and expenditures and establish a goal for profit. Achieving a profit is the fundamental challenge that all businesses in the free-enterprise system face. The budget that you set can be annual, monthly, weekly, or even daily. As your firm grows, budgeting will become more complex. But when it comes time to "cut the overhead," the budget will be a valuable tool in helping you understand your business operation and make "finding the fat" easier. An operating budget is just as important as any financial, legal, or design plan. Even when you are starting out, having a budget will help you measure your success and provide a roadmap to achieve your goals.

Chart 7 summarizes the major categories of monthly expenses that a design firm will encounter. Use it as a guideline to expand and refine as your new company grows!

CHART 7
Monthly Operating Expense Checklist

Expense	Estimated cost	Actual cost	Date to pay
Accounting/audit/tax			
Advertising			
Auto/gas/oil/repairs			
Auto registration/insurance			
Bank service charges			
Business entertainment			
CADD supplies			
Car payment			
Cell phone			
Computer lease			
Computer repair services			
Computer loans			
Contributions			
Conventions			
Copier lease			
Equipment rental			
Federal unemployment tax			
General office brochure			
Health insurance			
Internet connection			
Interest expenses			
Legal expenses			
Liability insurance			
Life insurance			
Miscellaneous licenses			
Bank loans			
Office supplies			
Other office expenses			
Payroll			
Payroll taxes			
Expense			
Photography			

(Continued)

Expense	Estimated cost	Actual cost	Date to pay
Postage/shipping/delivery			
Professional development			
Pension plan and trust			
Public relations			
Rent			
Repair/maintenance			
Retail sales tax			
State unemployment tax			
Temporary help			
Telephone			
Utilities			
Workers' compensation			
Total			

Use common sense. Ask yourself: "Does this expenditure make sense?"
Pass the decision by your "new business conscience" and ask: "Is this
expenditure good for the business?"

LEARN THE IMPORTANCE OF CASH

When you start your firm, you may invest not only your money (or other people's money) into the venture, but also those monies you will be receiving from your clients (accounts receivable). In business, it is very important to convert your accounts receivable into cash as quickly as possible. Why is that? The longer the money sits in your clients' pockets, the more expenses your firm will incur; and if the cash isn't there to pay the bills, stress sets in. You need money to pay for the operation of your company.

If the failure of design firms can be attributed to one major factor, it is the inability to manage accounts receivable. Remember the principals in your old firm discussing clients who did not pay for 90, 120, even 180 days? Designers are such good scouts when it comes to asking for money for services rendered that they end up defeating themselves. They are so sensitive; they don't want to offend the client. Asking for money may upset the client, and he may cancel the project, or get offended or angry with the designer. Besides, designers are concerned about design, not the dirty *M* word (money).

Well, forget all that—starting now! *Money for operations is more important than design in running a business.* "Blasphemy!" you say. Think of it this way: Sure, design is important and, yes, as a designer you are who and what you design. But what some designers fail to understand is that if they are slow in meeting their accounts payable, they may incur interest, which erodes the bottom line of profit of the firm. Further, they may get a bad credit rating. If the money isn't there to pay the consultants, vendors, employees, Uncle Sam, and your own salary, you will not remain in business very long. You will not be able to produce the design masterpieces that only you can create and be remembered for!

Cash is king in business.

To be a successful designer, you must be able to afford and pay your expenses. To help manage your cash flow, you need to develop a "seventh sense," a gut feeling about one vital sign of the business: the need for cash. This cash conscience will help you manage the business by knowing when to call clients for money to meet your need for cash (payroll, rent, insurance premiums, and so on).

How much operating cash does your business need? One rule of thumb is to take the average monthly budget for your new firm and divide it by twenty (the average number of business days in a month). The resulting figure is the "average" amount of cash that you should receive every business day.

Example. Your monthly operating costs are $8,000 (roughly a $96,000 to $100,000 per year business operation). You need to "average" $400 per day to operate. If you do not bill $8,000 for the month, you are losing money. If you do invoice $8,000 for the month, you will need to have approximately $400 per business day (or $2,000 per week, or $4,000 every two weeks) arrive in the mail or be delivered personally by clients. Now, in real life, $400 checks do not arrive in the mail day in and day out. Some days, no money will come in; other days, $2,000 will be realized! Some weeks you may get little cash, and others you may get flooded. Get a sense of when your expenses are due, and anticipate your cash flow around them. It's better to call a client a week in advance to receive money than to wait until a major account payable is due and interest is charged. Think about this vital sign—cash flow—on a daily basis. Anticipate cash, and if it doesn't arrive, demand it! You are due the money; you earned it.

Many designers agree that it is difficult to collect on delinquent client accounts—never mind asking for interest on balances past due. But when it comes to the bank, or to credit cards, they readily accept the interest charges of their own creditors. It seems that designers have established a standard that all client receivables are slow, and they do nothing to improve the situation. If you and your client agree that you will be paid in thirty days, demand payment on the thirtieth day. Set some goals. After you send your invoice, don't just bury your head in the sand like an ostrich and expect a payment check in thirty days! Produce the invoice—present it in person if possible. If you mail it, allow three business days, and then call your client to inquire if it was received. Ask if there are any questions about it, or any problems. Find out if you can expect payment according to the terms of your contract. It is much better to have this conversation now—and become aware of a potential cash shortfall because a client intends to pay in forty-five days instead of thirty—than to wait until the full thirty (or forty-five) days have passed! Don't be bashful. Believe it or not, clients will respect you for being conscientious about business concerns. It will further demonstrate your professional business skills and will cultivate clients with an understanding of their accountability and responsibility to you for services received.

Treat cash management with the same passion as design!

ESTABLISHING FEES

One of the most difficult issues to face and resolve in a start-up firm is how to "value" your services. What is your time worth to a client? Well, the answer to that question is very complicated.

When you worked for the firm that you interned with, you were probably exposed to the firm's billing rate structure, which on an hourly basis may have gone something like this:

Principal $150
Project manager $95
Project architect $75
CADD technician $60
Administrative staff $40

As an employee of the firm, you probably understood the rate differentials for various job classifications. A principal is of more economic value per hour than a draftsperson. But what may have made you curious is: How did the firm develop these hourly rates? Did it use some magical formula? Did it find out what the competition charges and develop equal rates? And why did the firm pay you $18 per hour while billing your time at $55 per hour? What happened to the other $37? Did the principals "pocket the money"?

The answer to all these questions is that a business has overhead, or costs associated with operating the business. (We will look at overhead later in this chapter.)

When you start your own firm, theoretically your overhead will be less than that of your former employer. For one thing, you may not be drawing a significant salary or paying a high rent (or any rent if you work out of your home). You may not have an expensive letterhead, an expensive phone system, a company car, and so on. Therefore, the costs of running your new firm could and should be less than that of your former employer.

This fact suggests that your standard hourly rates should be less than those charged by your former firm. Rates? Did I say *rates*? Why would you set several rates if "you" is only one person? The fact of the matter is that, in business, clients expect their consultants to be fair. Why should you charge clients $95 per hour to design or consult with them and then, when you return to your office, charge them the same $95 per hour to draft or prepare a specification? You must learn when you start your own firm that as the sole employee you need to wear many hats (or share them with a partner if you have one). Your value to a client is based upon which task you are performing. Use common sense! Why is a principal's hourly rate higher than a draftsperson's? Rate setting can be a frustrating exercise. However, to be successful you must value your time differently for each task that you perform.

WHAT SHOULD MY AVERAGE HOURLY RATE BE?

The simplest way to determine an average hourly rate is to ask yourself "What was my salary at my former job?" and work from there. Let's look at a simple case.

Example. Your employer is paying you $30 per hour in salary. There are two hundred workdays in a given year (excluding weekends and holidays and two weeks for vacation, if you even take one). The two hundred workdays equal

1,600 prime buffing hours, which translate into $48,000 annually. Now, this assumes that you will be working eight hours every workday on a project. Is that possible? The reality of it is that you will probably be working twelve to sixteen hours per day and close to three hundred days total in your first year! So the true translation is 3,600 to 4,800 hours. You will work this number of hours, first, because you will feel the need to and, second, because the risk of hiring another will appear immense. Therefore, you will accomplish the work of 2.25 people by yourself! Are you tired yet?

Whatever your former salary or total number of hours worked, as your own boss you now have additional costs to consider. What other tasks did you perform, and what other expenses did you incur, in completing a project for a client? Did you rent space for an office, did you buy paper, did you use electrical energy, did you drive to the client's office or home and use gasoline, do you have any insurance, and do you pay taxes? All these items swell the cost of doing business.

Again, when you start your new firm, your expenses should be minimal compared with those of other, established firms. Therefore, your hourly rate should be less. However, use common sense. If a client of your former employer asks you to do some work (does this sound familiar?), how much would you charge? To start with, you know what the market will bear. The client paid your former employer fees according to an approved hourly schedule. You could start off using the same rates. Some clients will pay those rates; others are more astute in business, understand overhead and opportunity, and expect or demand that your rates be significantly less. Know your market, understand the cost of running your business, and be fair. If you are lucky enough to have a client pay you the former firm's rates, you will be facing a very profitable project! Be smart and invest those profits in better equipment (computers, software, telephone equipment—anything to help make your job easier).

You will find that when you have to compete for a project against other firms, the price sometimes has an impact on the selection of a designer. Low-overhead firms with expertise will usually win!

Why do you think that in today's business climate all business-oriented firms are "right/down"-sizing? To control their overhead and become more competitive! Sure, it's tough to reduce staff and other business expenditures.

However, lean overhead results in higher profits for a company. Higher profits can mean bonuses, new equipment, capital reserves, peace of mind, and much, much more.

Remember, when you think of what your time is worth, take into consideration the following:

What costs are associated with doing this project?

My take-home
My expenses
Targeted profit

What will the market bear?

Understand that you will have to wear many hats. Be fair to yourself as well as the client!

WHAT IS OVERHEAD?

The principals of the firm that you worked for talked on and on about this "mystery term." You've heard it referred to as a number—perhaps two point five (2.5) or three point zero (3.0). You've heard endless talk about cutting overhead. You've wondered why the firm multiplied your hourly rate by a factor and charged the clients two or three times as much for your work. How could the firm do that? Where did all the other money go?

In simple terms, overhead refers to all costs associated with operating a business. All costs! Therefore, the lower the operating costs of your new company, the higher your profit will be on every dollar that you bill. Every city has architectural firms that operate in "high design" offices and those that work out of "slummy" offices. We all know the impact of image. But if your clients never come to your office, why spend a million dollars on expensive furniture and rent? When you are starting your firm, the lowest rent that you can pay is to operate out of your own home—unless of course you get an offer of "free" rent from some other source.

Chart 8 is an overhead costs checklist summarizing the types of expenses a design firm can expect to encounter. The next exercise to perform is to calculate how much of your overhead is attributable to direct costs of a project and how much is indirect, not chargeable to a project. You will find that most of your direct costs fall into the following categories:

Auto miles traveled to and from a project
CADD supplies directly attributable to a project
Office supplies directly attributable to a project
Payroll directly attributable to a project (normally 80 to 90 percent)
Postage/shipping/delivery directly attributable to a project
Photography directly attributable to a project
Telephone costs directly attributable to a project

Divide the direct costs into the indirect costs to find your firm's overhead factor:

$$\frac{\text{Indirect costs}}{\text{Direct costs}} = \text{Overhead factor}$$

Low overhead factors (ratios) are 1:1 or 1:2. Normal ratios for medium-sized firms are 1:4 to 1:6. Large firms have ratios of 1:5 to 1:75.

Let's return now to computing an "average" hourly rate to be charged by your new firm. First take your hourly salary rate of your current/former job and multiply it by the overhead factor to find your "payroll burden." Add the salary rate to that figure. Then multiply by a profit goal. The following example assumes an overhead rate of 1.3 and profit goals of 10, 15, and 20 percent:

Salary rate × Overhead rate = Payroll burden
$30.00/h   1.3 $39.00/h

Salary rate + Payroll burden = Salary + burden rate
$30.00/h $39.00/h $69.00/h

Salary + burden × Profit   = Hourly rate
$69.00/h   (10%)1.1 $75.90
                           (15%)1.15 $79.35
                           (20%)1.2 $82.80

Remember that this figure represents an average rate only. You will charge clients more for certain tasks and less for others. Now think about what all these computations mean in real terms. If you have a profit goal of 20 percent, and thus an hourly rate of $82.80, and if you put in 4,000 hours that first year, you will earn

Hourly rate × Hours × Profit goal = Earnings
$82.80   4,000   .20   = $66,240

A higher profit goal means higher earnings, of course—and you are your own boss!

CHART 8
Overhead Costs Checklist

Expense	Monthly cost	Annual cost	Percent
Accounting/audit/tax			
Advertising			
Auto/gas/oil/repairs			
Auto registration/ insurance			
Bank service charges			
Business entertainment			
CADD supplies			
Car payment			
Cell phone			
Computer lease			
Computer repair services			
Computer loans			
Conventions			
Copier lease			
Equipment rental			
Federal unemployment			
General office brochure			
Health insurance			
Interest expense			
Internet service			
Legal expenses			

(Continued)

Expense	Monthly cost	Annual cost	Percent
Liability insurance			
Life insurance			
Miscellaneous licenses			
Bank loans			
Office supplies			
Other office expenses			
Payroll			
Payroll taxes			
Postage/shipping/delivery			
Professional development			
Pension plan and trust			
Public relations			
Contributions			
Rent			
Repairs/maintenance			
Photography			
Retail sales tax			
State unemployment tax			
Temporary help			
Telephone			
Utilities			
Worker's compensation			
Total			

PROFIT

Profit is the reason you are in business. Great design is why you are in practice. Profit is your reward for taking the many business risks and resultant stresses that affect you from ownership. The standard acceptable profit margin for government projects is 10 percent. However, this should not keep you from setting a goal of a higher amount.

Many designers do not understand what profit is. The way they perceive profit is that it is the money left over at the end of the year after all the bills are paid! If they have some profit that is fine, and if they don't, maybe next year will be a better one. How naïve!

Profits, in reality, are monies left over after expenses. The strategy for a profitable design firm is to treat profit as an expense on a project. If your fee is $10,000 and you project a profit of $1,500, then attack the scope of work and do the project for $8,500. This will give you the profit you desire. Any time expended after $8,500 worth of services erodes the profit figure.

Looking at the big picture, if you need money from a bank for equipment or a line of credit, the bank wants to deal with a profitable business, not one in the red. It wants to diminish its risk.

Profit is the final score in the game of business.

Be careful not to give work away! Many designers do not recognize the big picture. They take on a project for what they think is "at cost," without profit, and do not understand how they end up losing money. Many take on multiple commissions this way, and if they do not properly manage the projects, they will go bankrupt in only a short time.

FINANCIAL RECORDS

When they start out on their own, most designers are likely to regard book-keeping as cruel and unusual punishment. They will do anything to avoid doing it. They will get anyone to do the books. It appears to be such a tiring, thankless task that most designers would actually go without records if they could get away with it. Design can be so freewheeling, and accounting has to be so exact! All the numbers in a column must add up.

Remember, your financial records are a critical tool in tracking the health and profitability of your firm. Review them as "snapshots" of given moments in time to evaluate your firm's performance. Use the records as guides to make decisions for the firm. Acknowledgment of the records as tools will help you learn from the past, understand the present, and forecast the future. Your financial records can help you plan your investments, fore-cast growth, and keep tax liabilities to a minimum. They are the keys to your firm's success.

When you start your firm, whether you incorporate or not, arrange your bookkeeping in a simple manner. Open a separate bank account for your busi-ness. Believe it or not, many consultants operate their businesses out of their personal accounts to "keep things simple"! This makes life difficult in tracking and controlling business funds.

Document all your expenditures, no matter how large or small.

This is the first law of record keeping! Document expenses by using checks and credit cards for all your payments. If you pay cash, limit it to smaller purchases and save the receipts! If you cannot obtain a receipt, document the purchase in some manner. Some businesspeople carry a separate notebook to keep tabs on their expenditures in the beginning. You will be amazed at how quickly the money goes out! And you will learn that cash goes out from the company easier than into it. The secret to a successful business is to have more money come in than goes out. That should be your first goal in accounting. Your new firm is not the federal government. You can't print money or spend more than you can raise. Therefore, always remember to spend less than you make. Use common sense!

BOOKKEEPING

When you start your firm, have your spouse, a friend, or an accountant "set up your books" (establish your accounting record formats) and explain the fundamental rules of accounting. If you are proficient on a computer, buy a basic accounting software package to get yourself started. Remember, keep it simple!

You may not need a sophisticated five-part software package specifically geared to a design firm. Many a firm was founded starting out with a "one write," single handwritten entry system or a simple bookkeeping record for the first year in business. Remember, let the bookkeeping system grow with your company. Don't overbuy!

When you start out, if you enjoy working with figures, by all means keep the books for your company. This is the best possible training in the business world. It will help you better understand the day-to-day activities required to run a business. If you can't stand working with figures, consider hiring a part-time bookkeeper. Consult with your accountant for a recommendation—accountants and bookkeepers often work as teams.

Look for these traits in a bookkeeper:

A good bookkeeper understands payroll/general ledger/accounts payable/accounts receivable, not just one or two of these categories.

A good bookkeeper keeps track of every penny.

A good bookkeeper doesn't settle for anything less than 100 percent accuracy when tallying a column of figures.

A good bookkeeper can analyze figures, not just record them.

A good bookkeeper will keep your business matters private.

A good bookkeeper will let you know when your expenses are greater than your income!

Remember, when you start out, you may need a bookkeeper only one day a week or three days a month. The amount of time will depend on your work volume. Some designers keep their own books for the first year to "learn the system" so that when they do hire a part-time bookkeeper, no one understands the business and its records better than they do.

Do I Need an Accountant?

The simple answer to this question in business is yes! An accountant is one of four essential business team advisers. (The others are your lawyer, banker, and insurance broker.)

A bookkeeper is not an accountant. Your accountant will provide many essential consulting services when you start your firm. He or she will:

Advise on organizational form (sole proprietorship versus partnership, etc.)

Advise on tax considerations (IRS forms, payments, etc.)

Coordinate with your attorney

Determine whether to use a cash or accrual method for keeping your books

Select a bookkeeping system (one-write, computer, etc.)

Consult on preparing a business plan

Help introduce you to bankers and lending institutions

Prepare profit and loss statements

Prepare a balance sheet

Prepare financial statements

Advise on tax strategies and planning

You need to meet with your accountant for only a few hours a year, but remember to schedule meetings regularly, perhaps each business quarter, to update the accountant on your business plans, projected revenues, and methods of operation. Discuss the details of your operation: how much money you want to make or spend, cash flow, taxes, financing, and so on. Don't expect profound advice from your accountant if you get together only once a year.

View your accountant as an important person who cares about your business and your success. Share confidences; discuss your concerns and problems. Above all, be prepared for your meetings. Accountants are not inexpensive. Present your information in a precise, economical, thoughtful way. Don't give information haphazardly and expect the accountant to understand the data in one sitting! Remember, accountants (bean counters) love organization and order. Giving accountants information in a disorganized fashion will cost you more money in the long run.

Select an accountant who has other designers for clientele. Such an accountant will understand your cost of doing business, and average profits, better than a novice accounting firm with no designer clients. An experienced accountant with design firms can "ramp up" with your new venture quicker than others. Accountants are business consultants, not just tax planners and filers. If you can't find an accountant who has experience with designers, call some of your colleagues or your designer association for references. Interview at least two or three firms to see if they are a "good match" for you. Don't hire a firm just on one referral. This firm will be responsible for helping you make money. You should like them and trust them. Consider retaining the services of a firm as experienced and passionate about what they do as you are about your new venture. Don't hire a "name firm" for the sake of their name. They may not service you in the way that you deserve. Don't be the accounting firm's largest client, nor its smallest one. Find one that can serve as one of your "mentors—showing you the ropes of business."

Call your accountant on a regular basis. Consider meeting with him or her quarterly to review your progress and to explain the impact on your "books," profit and loss statement, and balance sheet.

Also, if your accountant doesn't perform for you, fire him or her, and retain the services of another accounting firm. Most businesses treat accountants like internists and dentists. They never change, no matter what happens.

Make sure your accountant is up-to-date with tax laws that effect design firms, and that he or she treats you as if you matter. It is your money. It matters. You should matter.

SETTING UP A BASIC ACCOUNTING SYSTEM

A designer, like any businessperson, must keep accurate and thorough financial records for all income received and expenses incurred. It is that simple! The purpose of financial records is to help produce income, control expenses, track cash flow, keep tax payments to the legal minimum, and comply with other regulatory requirements.

Accounting is the theory and system of setting up, maintaining, and auditing the books of a firm; it is also the art of analyzing the financial position and operating results of a business from a study of its sales, purchases, and other transactions.

A good accountant will probably recommend that you do all of the following:

1. *Separate record keeping.* As stated earlier, it is essential to separate your business books from your personal records, checkbooks, and bank accounts. Financial statements will be easier to draft and financial applications will be simpler to execute. Most important, all business expenses will be traceable to one source. Personal draws are easily controlled and documented.

2. *Double-entry bookkeeping.* Most accountants prefer the double-entry bookkeeping system for maintaining business records. Transactions are entered first in a journal, and then monthly totals of the transactions are posted to one of five ledger accounts:

- Income

- Expense

- Assets

- Liabilities

- Net worth

Income and expense accounts are closed each year. Asset, liability, and net worth accounts are maintained on a permanent and continuous basis.

3. *Personal computer basic accounting software packages similar to QuickBooks.* There are dozens of basic accounting software packages available to the small start-up business. Look for one that is adaptable for a design (service) consulting firm.

In the beginning, remember to keep it simple. Some software packages will write all your checks, post the expenses, do payroll, and keep track of your receivables. As an extra bonus, they will produce trial balance sheets and income statements for your new enterprise. No matter how simple these packages may seem, before you purchase one (for as little as $39.95!), consult with other designers, ask your local Designer Association (AIA/ASID/NSPE) office if there is a users' group nearby, and buy a software consumers report to compare. Learn from others and their mistakes!

Remember, your start-up capital is essential, important, and scarce.

Don't spend a lot on a worthless program that is out of tune with your new design practice. Take your time, and look for the right fit for your needs!

If you are not comfortable with computers or accounting, think twice before you invest in software and a computer. Once you jump out of the airplane you'll have no time to teach yourself how to use a computer or software. It will eat up too much valuable time. If you think that you must have a computer and don't know how to use one, stay in the plane a little longer. Learn the system first, then jump!

Another consideration is to have someone whom you know and trust run your accounting software system at first, and teach you how to use it.

As designers, we may not know everything about architecture, interior design, or engineering, but we have been trained to "know enough to respect it and get by." We hire other design firms to produce work to supplement our design offering. The same needs to hold true for bookkeeping and accounting. You need to understand this topic. What better way than to get your hands dirty a little, and learn about this very important business topic, from your part-time bookkeeper and retained accountant. The more you learn from them, the more of a "business conscience" you will develop for your day-to-day efforts in your new design business venture.

CASH VERSUS ACCRUAL ACCOUNTING

Record-keeping systems differ in their basic methods of recording as well as in the amount of detail they show. These methods refer to the rules for computing "taxable income" and, more specifically, to the timing for recognition of specific items of income and deductions in a business for the Internal Revenue Service (IRS). Whether your books are single or double entry, you must choose between two accepted accounting methods: cash and accrual.

Under the cash method of accounting, income is recorded when cash (checks, money orders, or currency) is received, and expenses are recorded when paid. The cash system shows only what you have received, not what you have earned. Many design firms prefer this method because it reflects the fact that they pay taxes on the receivables they have received rather than earned.

The accrual method of accounting records all income and expenses, whether paid or not. This accounting system requires more bookkeeping effort than the cash method. However, most businesspersons prefer the accrual method because it provides a more accurate set of firm records. Bankers like businesses that use this method because it presents a "better picture" of the firm and its operation.

The Tax Reform Act of 1986 imposed strict limitations on the use of the cash method of accounting. Specifically, corporations and partnerships (other than S corporations and personal service corporations) must use the accrual method of accounting unless their average gross receipts for a three-year period do not exceed $5 million annually. Sole proprietorships, S corporations, and certain personal service corporations and partnerships may use the cash method of accounting. In practice, most companies continue to use the accounting method that appeared on their first tax return to the IRS.

The advantages and disadvantages of each system depend on your individual circumstances. Consult your accountant to assist you in making the correct choice.

DEPRECIATION

Throughout your new firm's lifetime, you will have to purchase property and equipment from time to time. This property will usually last for several years, so it is not reasonable to consider the whole cost as an expense in any given one-year time frame. Therefore, when the property or equipment is purchased, it is recorded in your financial records as a fixed asset or plant asset.

The decrease in value over the life of the asset, known as depreciation, is treated as an expense distributed over the time period during which the asset is used. There are several methods of computing depreciation. When figuring depreciation, you should consider the following factors:

Cost of the asset

Its estimated useful life

Estimated salvage or trade-in value at the end of its useful life

The simplest and most common way of computing depreciation is the straight-line method. Under this method, the estimated salvage value and any additional first-year depreciation taken are subtracted from the cost. The remainder is divided by the estimated useful life of the asset. The resulting figure is the amount to be charged as depreciation each accounting period.

Example. You purchase a PC for $1,500. Its salvage value is $500, and its useful life is five years. If straight-line depreciation is utilized, the annual depreciation is computed as follows:

$$\frac{\$1,500 - \$500}{5} = \$200$$

There are other methods of depreciation such as sum of *the years' digits* and *double declining balance*. You may choose different methods for different assets. For tax purposes, you must apply the same method to an asset over its useful life unless you obtain permission from the IRS.

Coordinate asset depreciation with the rest of your bookkeeping system. Let your accountant figure the method and record the data for your new firm.

LEARN THE BASIC IRS RULES FOR BUSINESS

Why should you, a designer, learn the basic IRS rules? The answer is a simple one. If you want to be successful in business and remain in business, you must acknowledge the existence of the IRS. Uncle Sam wants to share in your success.

To the average person, tax law is a complex headache—a nightmare. That's why accountants were created, right? Well, leaving all your tax work, planning, and filing to your accountant is fine. However, you should know some of the basics. In design school you learned how calculus was the basis of structural calculations, and as a designer you needed to be exposed to the theory. However, in practice there are people called structural engineers who will handle all such challenges. Similarly, you need to depend on an accountant to do the right thing for your new firm.

You may be a very proud person who has calculated all of your personal tax returns for years, knowing that you can figure out the tax forms as well as any accounting professional, and you do so to save money. In business, it is very different. The business side is so much more complex, with many different issues, forms, and time of year of filing requirements compared with just April 15 annually for your 1040 form. As I said earlier, know the basics of your business accounting, but allow the accountant tax professional to take over your tax filing requirements. Accountants know the ins and outs of the tax code far better than you do. You wouldn't allow them to design a space in their own building; why wouldn't you let them do all of your tax planning?

TAX LAWS

Many federal tax laws are designed solely to keep you from cheating Uncle Sam out of what he thinks is rightfully his: your company's money. Many other laws, however, are designed to save a company money by providing tax breaks. The IRS does make an effort to educate the public about taxes. But it is your responsibility as a taxpayer to investigate, understand, and file your taxes. Having a list of excuses for not filing on time is not good enough for the IRS.

One of the first things you need to do is to check out the IRS' Web site at *www.irs.gov*. This is a very user-friendly resource that has all the answers; it even has phone numbers to speak to a human being. The site to concentrate on is the Small Business and Self Employed One Stop Resource. It is well designed, with updates every year, and contains thorough explanations of income, excise, and employment taxes for all forms of businesses: sole proprietors, partnerships, and corporations. You will also need the appropriate tax forms. Every tax form created is identified on this Web site.

Accounting Period: Calendar Year versus Fiscal Year

Every business must keep financial records and file appropriate tax returns for a given taxable year, which is either a calendar year or a fiscal year. A calendar year begins on January 1 and ends on December 31. Make sure to check out the information on the IRS Web site about calendars. Most tax returns are due on April 15 (the fifteenth day of the fourth month following the end of the calendar year). Most small businesses use the calendar year—and the IRS prefers this format—because it is easier to contemplate. Most, if not all, of the IRS procedures are geared toward the calendar year.

A fiscal year is a twelve-month period ending on the last day of any month other than December. Fiscal year tax returns are due on the fifteenth day of the fourth month following the end of the fiscal year. There are strict, complex rules on who can conduct business on a fiscal year basis and when a decision must be made to adopt a fiscal year format.

Generally, sole proprietorships must use the same taxable years as those established by the founder/owner, which means the calendar year in the majority of cases. The same rule applies to partnerships, S corporations, and personal service corporations. However, the IRS will allow these forms of business to adopt a fiscal year format if there is a valid business reason for doing so. Regular corporations can choose either a calendar year or fiscal year format.

Why choose a fiscal year format? Some businesses have predictable annual cycles and find that coordinating their taxable year with those cycles better represents actual income and expenses for the business. Corporations often choose a fiscal year coinciding with their first month of operation in order to avoid a short-period tax return and extra taxes in the first year.

Again, discuss your options with your accountant before you start!

Who Must File Tax Returns?

This question used to have an easy answer. Times and taxes have changed. When in doubt, refer to the IRS Web site. Also, check out IRS Publication 501 on this topic. Remember, tax liabilities may change annually. Consult a current tax guide.

Every business must file a federal income tax return if net earnings from self-employment (business net profit) total $400 or more. (Business income minus expenses equals net profit.) For the Annual Tax Calendar for Calendar Year Businesses, refer to the IRS Publication 538 on the IRS Web site.

TYPES OF TAXES
Income Taxes

The type of federal income tax return you are required to file will depend on the form of business you undertake. If you operate as an individual proprietorship (you are the sole owner and the business is not incorporated), you must report your business operations on Schedule C and attach it to Form 1040, your individual tax return.

If you operate as a partnership, the business must file a Form 1065. The partnership is not liable for federal income tax. However, the partners must report their share of profits or losses on their individual Form 1040.

If you operate as a corporation, the corporation must file a Form 1120 and pay taxes on the taxable income reported. If you receive any salary or dividends from the corporation, you must report them on your individual Form 1040. Gross dividends over $400 must be listed separately on Schedule B, which is filed with the individual return.

Corporation tax returns are due on the fifteenth day of the third month following the close of the firm's taxable year. Individual and partnership returns are due on the fifteenth day of the fourth month. Never assume due dates with the IRS! Always coordinate the requirements with your accountant. Once you start this cycle, you must stay with it annually.

Self-Employment Tax

Self-employment tax represents social security payments for self-employed individuals. Independent businesspeople pay the highest social security rate of all (since they must make both the employer's and the employee's contribution), and the maximum increases every year. Self-employment tax is imposed on the taxable income (net profit) of your business. It is apart from and in addition to your federal income tax liability.

Sole proprietors and partners are liable for self-employment tax. Corporate stockholders are not. Self-employment tax is filed with your regular federal income tax return, using Schedule SE.

Estimated Income Tax

If your federal tax liability for a current year (income plus self-employment combined) is estimated to be $500 or greater, you may be required to pay your tax in quarterly installments to the IRS. Like taxes withheld from employees' paychecks, the government wants its share in advance.

Quarterly payments are due on April 15, June 15, September 15, and January 15. You do not have to pay the fourth estimate as long as you file your return by January 31 and pay the balance due.

How do you estimate your taxes? You have two options. First, you can base your estimate on the amount of taxes that were due on your last tax year's income, divide it by four, and send that amount to the IRS every quarter. Second, you can estimate your taxes on the basis of your current income in this tax year. Each quarter, you figure your taxable income and send the IRS the correct tax. Be careful of this method, because the IRS can levy an interest penalty if you underestimate your income by more than 10 percent. Also, if you pay three low quarterly payments and you have a profitable year, beware of the tax-bite on April 15! You may have to make a whopper payment.

If you are a sole proprietor or partner, you are liable for estimated tax. Payments are submitted on a four-part form, 1040-ES. If you underpay your estimated taxes, you may be subject to a penalty and/or interest charges because the IRS wants its tax dollars sooner rather than later. This is a major reason to have a professional accountant assist you on your business matters. Should a problem arise with your tax calculations, your accountant can represent you and your business interests to the IRS.

Payroll Taxes

If your new firm has any employees, you will have certain obligations to the IRS for payment of payroll taxes and withholding of income taxes related to your employees' salaries in a given tax year. Similarly, you will probably have a tax-withholding obligation to your state and maybe your local jurisdiction. Discuss your obligations with your accountant!

Although the IRS does not prescribe any particular form in which your payroll records must be kept, you should incorporate the following as good practice:

◆ Each employee's name, address, and social security number.

◆ The amount and period of each wage payment.

* The amount of wages subject to withholding, included on each wage payment.

* The amount of tax withheld and date collected.

* Your employer identification number. (If you do not have one, call the IRS and obtain Form SS-4 to file for one.)

* Duplicate copies of all returns filed.

* Dates and amounts of deposits made with the IRS.

* Your employees' withholding exemption certificates (Form W-4).

There are three types of federal payroll taxes that you must withhold:

Income taxes
Social security taxes (FICA)
Federal unemployment taxes (FUTA)

Income taxes. Income taxes are withheld on all wages paid to an employee above a determined minimum. The minimum is governed by the number of withholding allowances claimed by the employee.

Income tax deposits are made to the IRS and your state through your bank. Depending on the amount, the taxes may be collected quarterly, monthly, or biweekly. The requirements for due dates are complex and should be coordinated with your accountant.

Social security taxes (FICA). Social security taxes apply to a portion of wages paid to an employee during a particular tax year. Recently, the portion has been raised each year, so you should coordinate the current requirements with your accountant. The amount withheld from the employee's wage is matched by the company as the total tax.

Federal unemployment taxes (FUTA). During the tax year, employers are required to pay FUTA taxes on each employee's first $7,000 of wages paid. You may receive a credit against your federal unemployment taxes for a certain percentage of the state unemployment taxes you pay. FUTA taxes are explained in depth on IRS Form 940.

State Taxes

Many states collect income taxes and have procedures and rules similar to federal regulations.

State income taxes, like federal income taxes, are based on your net income or net profit. Most states simply compute state tax as a percentage of the income shown on your federal return. Generally, you are allowed the same deductions and expenses that the feds allow. It is important to coordinate your state tax liability, strategy, and form processing with your accountant.

Also, be careful with state sales tax laws. As a design firm, you are subject to audit by your State Sales Tax Department to determine if you owe the state any sales tax on items sold or services rendered. Each state is different. Make sure you discuss this topic with your accountant. It is very important, and oftentimes overlooked.

THE IRS AND YOU

The previous paragraphs should help you understand why a general knowledge of the IRS and its internal workings will benefit you in your dealings with the government. More than likely, like the majority of individuals and businesses filing returns, you will never get audited. The fact of the matter is that the IRS audits less than 2 percent of all tax returns filed.

All federal returns are automatically checked by computer for errors. If one is found, it does not increase your chances of an audit. What is important to remember is that returns that are audited are those that are obviously out of line with the IRS' idea of the "norm." When returns are recorded on computer tape for archiving at the regional IRS service centers and then sent to the national computer center in Martinsburg, West Virginia, they are inspected and compared with what is known as the DIF (discriminate input function) formula. This DIF is a computer program of the average American's financial profile. If your return is within the DIP formula, you are deemed an honest taxpayer, and you will probably never hear from the IRS about your return. If your return is outside the DIF, IRS agents will review it, and if they think the return is a potential money-maker for the government, they will audit you.

You can generally expect the IRS to look at the following items on your return:

Unusual or unreasonable business expenses
Large deductions for entertainment
An unreasonable profit, comparing total expenses with total income
Inconsistency from one year to the next

Discuss these items with your accountant, and get his or her opinion and recommendations on them as well as on other matters. Chart 9 lists typical business expenses that are allowable as IRS deductions.

CHART 9
Typical Business Expenses Allowable as IRS Deductions

Accounting fees
Accounting records format
Advertising
Auditing fee
Automobile expenses

Bad debt expenses
Bank service charges
Bookkeeping services
Books with useful life of one
    year or less
Business associations
Business cards
Business gifts
Business licenses

Charitable contributions
Cleaning expenses
Coffee service
Collection expenses

Consultant fees
Conventions
Credit card fees

Depreciation
Dues: business associations/
    professional societies

Education expenses
Electricity
Employer's taxes
Entertainment
Equipment

Insurance
Interest on business debt

Janitorial services

Legal expenses
License fees

Magazines

Minor repairs

Moving expenses

Office furnishings

Office in the home

Office supplies

Passport fees (for business trip)

Payroll and withheld payroll
  taxes

Periodicals

Postage

Property taxes

Rent

Safe deposit boxes

Salaries

Security system monitoring
  services

State income tax

Stationery

Supplies

Telephone

This book!

Travel away from the office
  on business

Utilities

Any significant changes in your return from year to year will invite an IRS review—and possible audit. If you ever had the pleasure of an IRS audit, or experience one in the near future, your chances of being audited again increase. The IRS, unlike lightning, does strike the same person twice—or even more!

Declaring a business loss on your tax return does not automatically cause an audit. A loss, however, will more likely be examined by the IRS. It is common for companies with large start-up costs and slow business to report a loss in their first year. However, after the first year, if a business shows continued losses, and does not show a profit for at least three out of five consecutive years, the IRS has the power to determine that the business is a "hobby" and to disallow any losses. IRS agents will allow ongoing losses if they are convinced during an audit that the taxpayer is operating a real business and trying to make a profit.

FAILURE TO FILE A RETURN

In today's world of computers, the IRS isn't infallible, and it isn't Big Brother looking over your shoulder. The IRS doesn't know everything! Why, then, bother to file a return, especially for incidental income?

In the design business, there is a reasonable chance that you have conducted some moonlight work for smaller projects during your tenure at your current or former employer. If you didn't (or do not) report this income to the IRS, you failed to file a comprehensive, accurate return. You realized financial gain, and Uncle Sam didn't share in it!

Some clients may want to pay for your services in cash, thus eliminating any paper trail for money spent and avoiding tax liabilities. Be careful! Only you can make the decision on whether to accept this form of compensation. It is tempting to say yes and not record or report the income. This is being intentionally dishonest, and may lead to further problems. If you elect to accept cash for payment of services, treat it similarly to tips received by waiters and waitresses. Report the income on Form 1099 as a supplement to your W-2 form from your employer.

As a moonlighter, you might work for years and receive $5,000, $10,000, or $20,000 in overtime pay. If you do not report the income and the IRS audits you and finds out, look out! You will be subject to pay all back taxes plus penalties and interest accrued: a no-win situation. Be careful, and think twice before conducting work without paying taxes. Finally, make sure you save all your tax returns. Inevitably, whenever you have the future need for capital, your potential banker will request several years of returns for review.

The basic rules to remember with the IRS are the following:

* Know the filing dates for your business's taxable year.

* Document every expenditure and income source as if you expected an audit notice from the IRS tomorrow.

* Don't miss a payment, because if you do, it takes forever to get out of the IRS computer.

* The IRS is always right, most of the time!

Don't be fearful of the IRS. Instead, use it as a motivating factor, a prod to your business conscience, to keep accurate and documented records.

You must have a professional accountant tax advisor to assist you through the myriad of the sales and income tax landscape. Ask questions.

Sign the forms, write the checks, send them in, and get on with your design business!

As the old saying goes, "The more successful you are financially, the more taxes you are liable for." Seek assistance to retain as many of your hard-earned dollars as possible in your pocket, and not in Uncle Sam's. Pay your fair share, and move on.

6
BANKING CONSIDERATIONS

"*A bank is a place where they lend you an umbrella in fair weather and ask for it back when it begins to rain.*"

—ROBERT FROST

"*If you owe the bank $100 that's your problem. If you owe the bank $100 million, that's the bank's problem.*"

—J. PAUL GETTY

"*A bank is a place that will lend you money if you can prove that you don't need it.*"

—BOB HOPE

I'll never forget the couple of days before I officially opened my new company's doors. I went to the "big" bank on the corner and asked for the necessary forms to open a new commercial checking and savings account. When I told the banker that I had $200 to put in both accounts, I was advised to "come back when you have more money"! Then I went down the street to the other "big" banks, and I couldn't believe that they said the same thing. Here I was, experiencing one of the most incredible highs of my life, starting my own firm, and boy did those bankers blow my ego!

I then got some advice from a business friend to talk to his banker, who was with a smaller bank and related well with start-up businesses. When I met with this "smaller banker," I was very careful not to take out my frustrations on him, but also I was

> *concerned about "going down in flames" again. I decided to level*
> *with him, and after ten minutes my new firm had two bank*
> *accounts confirmed on a handshake with my new banker. I will*
> *never forget him, because he listened to me, understood my con-*
> *cerns, and believed in me.*

Your relationship with your bank is your financial lifeline. The process of selecting a bank (and a banker) is a critical one, and you should discuss your firm and business plan with at least six institutions before you select one.

Ask your accountant and lawyer which bank and bankers they recommend. These are probably the most effective introductions. If a banker has an ongoing relationship with a professional who is advising you as a client, a less impersonal relationship will exist, and there is a better chance that more careful decisions will be made about your needs. Rely on your network of contacts.

Try to select a bank and banker who do business with other design professionals, because they will be experienced with design business matters.

Also, select a bank that has a branch close to your office, so that you can more easily conduct your banking transactions.

BANKING SERVICES

When you are selecting a bank for your new firm, consider the services offered. Sure, on the surface, all banks appear to be full-service. What does "full" mean? Compare the services of each candidate bank. You may be surprised at what you find. Each bank may treat a particular service differently.

Also, investigate the fees associated with banking services. Does the bank charge a fee for check writing? Deposits? (Imagine, some banks charge you to deposit money in their bank!) Monthly savings accounts? Are there any limitations on how many checks you can write per month on a particular account? The following are standard services offered by most banks for start-up businesses:

Online banking
Commercial checking accounts
Small business checking accounts
Business savings accounts

Commercial money market accounts
Payroll accounts
Cash management services
Short-term loans
Long-term loans
Lines of credit
Letters of credit
Automatic teller machine (ATM) usage

Take your time when evaluating candidate banks and their services. Make sure the bank's service offerings meet or exceed your new firm's banking requirements. There is nothing worse than having a bank that doesn't understand your business, that cannot or will not help you grow. Further, it is frustrating if your bank is too big and treats you and your firm as "small potatoes."

Before you meet with any bankers, it is important to understand where bankers come from. They are trained to be skeptical and always require two sources of repayment on loans. The primary sources of repayment are cash flow for short-term loans and earnings for long-term loans. All deals with bankers are backed up with some form of collateral such as accounts receivables or assets. Then, if something goes wrong with the original payment plan, the banker always has at least one fall-back position.

When you are starting your firm, the first rule in selecting a financial institution is: pick a banker, not a bank. As we discussed in the selection process for lawyers and accountants, you should select a banker who is genuinely interested in your new firm and understands architecture and the practice of it.

The second rule is as follows: Every loan officer in a bank is a vice president; therefore, forget big titles and pick a young, aggressive loan officer and gain his or her confidence. How do you gain the confidence of the loan officer? The first rule of "selling the banker" is to exhibit confidence in yourself as well as your new company. Bankers thrive on track records, so when you are starting out with no record, you may feel it is an impossible feat to sell the bank. This is where your self-confidence and communication skills come in. Both will play an integral part in the future success of your firm. Before you meet and interview potential banks and loan officers, you must do your homework. When you visit each bank, have the following information with you:

Preliminary business plan
Preliminary marketing plan
Your current résumé
Projected operating budget

Leave copies of these with all your potential lenders, even if you are not asking for a loan and are just inquiring about opening a commercial checking and savings account. You will be perceived as being extremely organized and confident, and thus a lesser risk to the bank. That is what banking is all about—it is a game of risk. Banks sell money and services that deal in money.

The third rule to follow when you visit the banks is to remember that you are doing banks a favor by bringing your new enterprise to them. Banks may control all the money, but without you and your new firm, they can't make any money on their money!

The fourth rule is to make your potential banker your silent partner. Sell your banker on the fact that your new firm is viable and potentially profitable, and that you may not need loan capital at this stage, but you do need the bank's expertise in helping you operate and grow. You will be surprised how many banks, especially the big ones, do not want to help small businesses (not to mention new design service businesses) start out. They feel that they will lose money because the new ventures will need only checking accounts and will maintain minimal savings accounts. Also, do not be surprised if a bank extends an offer to your new company contingent on gaining all your personal banking requirements.

Once you make a decision and select your new banker and bank, you'll quickly learn that they will expect you to personally countersign for any loans that you ask for. Don't let this throw you. How many people do you know that say they would never sign any such thing? They would sign only "unsecured" loans. Well, the fact of the matter is that when the bank asks you to personally guarantee a loan request, it's the only way it has to certify your numbers and your confidence in what you are doing. Asking for a loan is a double-edged sword. Don't take the responsibility lightly. It's easy for any new firm to be overly optimistic. Before you sign that note, read all the fine print and take a good hard look at all the figures. Your signature is more than an autograph!

Bank policies change from time to time, and a design firm can be looked upon as an increasing risk. If the real estate market is in a slump, for example, your bank could make a policy decision to be very cautious about existing or pending loans related to real estate deals. Therefore, since you as a designer deal in the real estate industry, your banking relationship could be adversely affected. If you think the bank is concerned, prepare a realistic assessment and business plan of how you intend to deal with the situation.

WHAT DO BANKERS KNOW ABOUT THE DESIGN BUSINESS?

Most new design firms start when the overall economy is weak or in a stage of recovery, or when the economy is overwhelmingly strong. Bankers have little information available to them regarding the basic characteristic of design firms and their financing needs. Lenders usually pay specific attention to the following characteristics of a firm:

Firm reputation
Variety of client base
Cash flow patterns
Insurance coverage

Most design firms are small and privately held. Of the more than 100,000 design firms in the United States, few are publicly held. The reason is that design firms are labor-intensive and usually operate with a staff of fewer than fifty employees to maintain control. Also, managers of design firms typically prefer more professional autonomy than their counterparts in larger firms. Small design firms need less financing in the initial stages of operation because they are primarily leveraging up managerial talent.

The capital structure of design firms varies with the type of organization. Sole proprietorships and partnerships rely extensively on the owner's capital. Historically, start-up firm owners and partners have been reluctant to relinquish the autonomy that comes with limited credit restrictions imposed by banks; therefore, many new firms are undercapitalized. The design profession in general, being labor-intensive, allows for small and thinly capitalized operations.

Bankers pay special attention to the owner's reputation and background of experience.

Start-up design firms usually have two strikes against them in applying for loans with banks. First, they do not provide a standardized product or service. Second, the owner is usually considered a designer—that is, someone who is technically competent, but has no formal financial or management training.

Bankers realize that many new design firms begin as spin-off companies. The founder is a classic entrepreneur who is not always motivated by profits but whose mission in life is to implement his or her ideas in a way that could not be done in the old firm. Client loyalty—the focus of the marketing plan—relies heavily on the reputation of the firm as a whole, and in many cases on the individuals within the firm. Many a new firm's portfolio is comprised of contracts with clients from the owner's prior place of employment.

The geographic locale of a design practice also has an impact on how bankers view the new business. It has been estimated that the western and southern regions of the United States will experience the greatest population growth in the future. In reviewing a credit application, many a banker analyzes the relationship between the range of services the design firm expects to provide and the local demand environment evidenced by demographic trends.

Insurance coverage also plays a major role in a banker's review of a new firm. Many new firms intentionally plan to "go bare"—that is, not carry professional liability insurance. Many banks will view this as poor risk management, and will allow the firm to have checking and savings accounts but will not provide any credit line because of the potential liability exposure. Commercial banks may require new firms with partners to carry key person insurance, designed to cover lost billings if a key individual leaves the firm or dies. In the case of death, the insurance also covers the stock liquidation payments.

Because reputation and referral commissions are critical to a design firm, loan officers will check the reputation of your firm and its individual registered professionals. They will contact local licensing boards to verify licensure and the existence of any record of reprimands. They will check with suppliers and consultants with whom they have a banking relationship as to your firm's credibility and creditworthiness.

Finally, bankers will evaluate the mix of business or clients that you have. If you have one large client, or only one client, don't expect a loan. The bank will ask the logical question: "What if your client goes bankrupt? How will you repay your loan if you lose all your business?" Lenders are "risk averse." As with your stock portfolio, the more diverse your clientele list, the better. Don't have all your eggs in one basket with one stock; diversify so that you have numerous baskets in which to place your eggs.

WHAT CHARACTERISTICS DO BANKERS LOOK FOR IN A NEW DESIGN FIRM?

As stated in the preceding section, start-up firms usually have a few "strikes" against them with bankers when it comes to creditworthiness. New design firm owners typically come to a bank when they have no track record or history in the field as business owners.

Here are a few things that bankers evaluate when they are approached for credit:

- Bankers prefer that a new owner operate the particular firm for at least a year prior to approaching the bank. During this time, the new firm will have developed a clientele and referral network. Bankers recommend that during this first year, the new firm save money to help support itself. Banks prefer not to provide funds to pay the salaries of owners.

- Bankers like to see a new firm rely on an accountant and a lawyer for assistance in developing business projections and business plans. Bankers are more comfortable when you bring these professional advisors with you to talk to them.

- Bankers look for a sound second source of repayment of the credit amount, should the firm fail. This second source could be inside or outside the company (e.g., a strong co-borrower, your house, your stock portfolio, your parents, your personal assets). The source can be waived in the future when the company grows stronger.

- The company and owner should be of upstanding character— honorable and trustworthy. Bankers want to know how you will react when times get tough. They want to know as much as they can about who you are as a person. Remember, they are risk averse. They deal in money, and they want it all back over time, with interest. That is how they make their profit.

* The customer must have the capacity to repay the loan. If your company is not profitable or has poor cash flow, chances are the bank will not extend credit. Remember, banks are in the business of lending money and getting paid back!

* The borrower should be adequately capitalized. This can provide the necessary cushion to help protect the bank if the firm fails or if business and economic conditions change. Banks look at savings accounts, stock portfolios, the cash value of insurance policies, and so on.

* Bankers like collateral. Having a tangible asset backing up each loan means that if anything goes wrong with the loan, the bank is covered.

Bankers review the above items as tried-and-true rules of good loan making. They are the core of sound commercial banking.

You will learn several things quickly if you deal with bankers:

Bankers will not be complacent in reviewing your account. They will review it at a minimum on an annual basis.

They will not be careless. There will be many "eyes" in the bank to review your account.

Bankers love to communicate and watch over your shoulder. They will be clear and concise with their information for you.

They will evaluate the competition of other banks, but not get carried away by it, because there will always be other businesses that need cash and credit.

Now that you have some understanding of bankers and what they look for in a new business, its accounts, and potential credit, how do you apply for a loan?

APPLYING FOR A LOAN

Many designers have a difficult time asking for money, whether it is from clients or from their banker. The idea of "going into debt" for this new venture may be challenging to you. Owing people money is a responsibility that cannot be taken lightly.

Why would you need a loan to start your business? To have start-up capital for salaries and/or to outfit and create a new business space are a few reasons. Don't borrow money in the beginning if you don't have a reason to. Create "sweat equity" in your business by working as much as you can with yourself and your time, not other people's money. Many businesses cannot start up without "start-up capital." Many founders have saved money over time, and have elected to use this cash as their start-up capital. Be fair to yourself. If you act as a bank to yourself, make sure that you pay yourself back over time for the "loan" you made to your company. You can be more forgiving and understanding to yourself than to the bank.

Getting a loan from a lender is a matter of selling yourself, and the better prepared you are, the more likely you are to be successful. Remember, you cannot assume that bankers will know everything about your firm, and it is your job to educate them. You begin this educational process by submitting a loan proposal containing the following items:

- Loan request
  - Purpose of the loan
  - Amount required
  - Term desired
  - Source of repayment
  - Collateral available

- History and nature of the firm
  - Two brief paragraphs
- Updated business plan
- Financial budgets (projected)
- Financial information
  - Balance sheet/income statement
  - Personal financial statement

If you present this information in an organized fashion, you will be amazed at the favorable and enthusiastic response you will get from your banker! Why? Because only the top 1 percent of the bank's customers ever do such a thing. Your banker will be quite impressed. You will give the impression that you really know what you are doing and you will get what you ask for. Treat this exercise like a presentation of a conceptual design to a client: It is an exciting time for the project; you are proud of the product and will do everything in your power to convince the client to approve the design. Bring this same excitement to the banker's table, convincing the bank that it is helping not only your company but itself, because the loan will make your firm more profitable and thus develop the need for further growth and an expanded banking relationship.

Your banker will evaluate your loan request according to five Cs:

1. Character. Who are you? If you are not someone to be trusted, then the bank won't deal with you. This criterion is by far the most important.

2. Capacity. What is your financial strength and track record?

3. Capital. How much of your own money do you have invested?

4. Collateral. What is available to support the primary source of repayment?

5. Conditions. What is the economy doing and how will it affect your firm?

BANK ETIQUETTE

Finally, here are some dos and don'ts that will strengthen your banking relationship:

Do

Make regular appointments and allocate enough time to meet with your banker.

Shoot straight; be honest.

Do your homework.

Ask questions if you do not understand anything.

Prepare a definitive business/banking needs plan.

Be flexible.

Always get your annual tax return forms and annual financial statements in on time. This impresses upon the banker/lender that you are on top of things and a real businessperson.

Don't

Be impatient.

Make promises that you can't keep.

Ask "how much" you can borrow.

Spend the money before you ask for it.

Ever surprise your banker.

Ever be late with a loan payment. If you have to be, due to cash flow issues, call your banker and explain the circumstances. If you call in advance, most bankers will appreciate your candor and work with you on the payment options. If you are going to be late and do not communicate to the banker, your credit will suffer.

7
MARKETING CONSIDERATIONS

"Business has only two functions—marketing and innovation."
—MILAN KUNDERA

"The aim of marketing is to know and understand the customer so well the product or service fits him and sells itself."
—PETER F. DRUCKER

If I am going to be working sixteen hours a day, and I have enough work to keep myself busy, when do I market for the next job? How can I do two things at once: draw at my desk and market? What is marketing, anyway? How can I promote myself if I am stuck at the office, or on a job site, or traveling all day? Where is the next project coming from?

I started my firm two years ago, and I was so focused on getting the work done that I never took the time to go after new work, because I just didn't have the time. When I completed the construction documents on that project, I had nothing else to do other than put the original project out to bid and await the construction phase. I guess I need to go out and market some more work!

We were so busy and committed to getting this large project done over the past six months that we didn't spend any time going after new work. When we completed the project's construction documents, our client went bankrupt. We had no other work to design at the time and were going to have a difficult time being paid for the work on the bankrupted project, so we had to close down our practice to pay the bills. I'll never do that again!

HOW ARE YOU GOING TO MARKET YOUR NEW FIRM?

Besides working on your first commission and writing a few checks to pay your start-up bills, somewhere along the line you must spend time focusing on what you want to do and how you plan to do it.

Since designers are deadline-oriented and predominately procrastinators, they rarely take the time to plan and be proactive in marketing. Instead, they practice daily crisis management, putting out one fire after another. Who has time to think, let alone plan? The fact of the matter is that if you force yourself to take the time in the evening or on the weekend—time away from the prime forty-hour week—to plan your new firm's direction, and step back every now and then to analyze and measure your charted course, you will be very successful in doing work that you like to do.

Now that you have your new headquarters and you are armed to the teeth with your weaponry for business, how are you going to market all this? When you worked at the old firm, all you did was design, or do production drawings, or construction administration, or maybe all three. What did the principals or marketing staff do? How did they market to bring in new work for employees to work on? How do you learn to market? What does it take to market? How will you market your new firm and the services it provides?

Will you like marketing? Do you have to do it, or can you expect someone else to do it?

Do you know the difference between selling and marketing?

WHAT IS MARKETING?

Marketing is an essential process for success in the design business. It is a process that involves a wide spectrum of activities, both direct and indirect, with the ultimate goal of convincing clients that you and your firm are sensitive to their needs, and can be trusted to solve their design challenges and be retained under contract to do so. Marketing is not sales.

There are only two kinds of marketing: direct and indirect.

You engage in direct marketing when you become aware of a particular project, write the requisite letter, make the necessary phone call, go and visit the potential client, and hope for an interview and selection. Direct marketing is having one-on-one contact with the potential client, either face to face or via written or verbal communication.

Direct marketing can be both reactive and proactive. An example of "reactive direct marketing" would be: You are notified by a friend that a particular business is planning to expand their retail space. You are given the name of the person who owns the business and who will make the decision to engage the designer needed. You contact that person (lead) directly, either by calling him on the phone and speaking with him directly or leaving him a voice mail, sending him an e-mail, writing him a letter, or paying him a visit in his current retail space. In other words, you react to the referral by attempting to discuss the project with him directly.

An example of being proactive in direct marketing would be: You know that one of your strengths is in retail space design. Rather than wait for prospective clients to call you, or have others refer you, you decide to be proactive, and contact many potential retail customers via written or verbal means. You may target this select group by sending e-mails about your business, sending a small brochure on your retail experience, or even stopping in their stores to discuss their future needs for space if they need any. This type of marketing is directly communicating with the potential prospects in a proactive manner in which you create, control, monitor, measure, and follow up to develop new business.

You engage in indirect marketing in literally everything else you do, from the moment you arise in the morning until you retire in the evening. You market indirectly by going to church, shopping for food, attending a little league baseball game, or making a deposit at the bank. The importance of indirect marketing is that you never know whom you will meet. Anyone could be a potential client or referral. Someone could just pop up on the same social, professional, or building committee. You market indirectly every waking hour of the day. This also holds for any partner(s) you may have. In fact, any employee whom you engage in the future will be an ambassador of the firm.

Studies have shown that indirect marketing is more important than direct marketing to a design firm because most of its commissions come through a contact referral network or through the recommendations of satisfied clients.

Many designers fail in business because of poor marketing. Some do not appreciate the necessity of marketing; others do not know how to market. Some do not like to market and still others do not want to market. If you fit into one or more of these categories, make sure you find a partner who doesn't. Or just learn to tolerate marketing and do it, because if you don't, failure is not far around the corner.

In a start-up firm, it can be challenging to have two or more partners focused only on marketing. While bringing in the work is important, someone has to be in the office producing it. There must be balance between the partners. Getting the work is the most important variable in the design business equation. If there is no new work, nothing will be accomplished.

Don't fall into the trap of getting that first and second design commission, only focusing on getting the design and production work done, and ignoring direct and indirect marketing. While you have a commitment to your new customers with your design contracts, you also have a commitment to your firm to continue providing new work to maintain a healthy business.

SHOULD YOU CONSIDER RETAINING A MARKETING CONSULTANT?

Many designers who do not enjoy marketing, or who feel they do not have good marketing skills, think that the answer is to hire a full-time marketing person to fill the void. Many expect a marketing expert to provide new projects within a short period of time. The fact of the matter is that potential clients must be cultivated. Marketing seeds take many months, if not a year, to germinate once they are planted. Marketing consultants are indirect, long-term salespeople for a firm, not short-term solutions for business development. Marketing consultants are not sales people. People in sales are normally promoting a tangible product, rarely a service. Marketing people promote a service firm's existence and offerings. They rarely close a deal.

Marketing consultants can help you focus on strengthening your marketing skills. They can write press releases and distribute them to newspapers and magazines. They can prepare brochures or edit newsletters for the firm. And they can help you develop a contact network for future prospects. Most important, they can help you forge the correct image for your new firm and show you how to communicate it to the outside world.

Marketing consultants cost money. For a start-up firm, a full-service consultant may be unaffordable. However, consider retaining one on an hourly basis to help you focus on your immediate, midrange, and long-term marketing goals. Later on in this section you will learn how to develop a preliminary marketing plan. Review your initial draft with a marketing consultant for an outsider's opinion.

As your company grows and changes, your needs for a marketing consultant will evolve. If you elect to retain the services of one, schedule quarterly meetings to review your firm's progress and monitor and record your marketing goals.

IMAGE

A major issue that you must address—whether alone, with your partner(s), or with a marketing consultant—is what image you want your new firm to have. Image is directly related to the vision that you have for the firm and its future. Whatever vision you have, the image must be consistent, or you will not get on track and achieve the results you need for success. Your thoughts on "image" affect every decision that you make in the day-to-day operation of your firm.

Some designers set too high an image, one that they cannot afford to obtain or maintain. A designer with aspirations to create residential architecture certainly does not need the same image as a healthcare designer who wants to design large hospital projects. Similarly, if you work alone, you do not need the image of a five hundred–person firm!

Image is projected in your company's name and letterhead, in your office, even in the clothes you wear. Like it or not, your behavior, your appearance, and the image of your firm are all impressions on which the world will judge you as you make the journey toward success in business and in life.

One of the challenges you will face at the outset is that if your markets are varied, you will need to be flexible and project different images. For many designers who have only one market, this is not a problem. However, if an opportunity occurs outside your niche, you must make a careful decision. Do you belong in that particular market? Can you be successful in it? If you get involved in it, where might it lead you? How does it compare with your current market(s)? Will it mix in well? Are you qualified to do a project in the new market, or will you consider hiring another to produce the project? Sounds complicated, doesn't it?

Most new firm owners are entrepreneurs who do not like to say no to opportunities. They see a particular project as income, and say yes without considering the big picture. If you are an owner who can't say no to opportunities, get ready for a complex, potentially schizophrenic marketing experience. Your firm may have a variety of images, and you'll need to dress for success in each different arena.

As an entrepreneur firm leader, you emit a "perception" to those who meet you or view you as a person. As the saying goes, "you only get one chance for a great first impression." Your behavior, your attire, and your grooming habits all say a lot about you to others. Make sure that your "physical image" is consistent with the type design firm that you lead. Make perceptions realities. Be consistent. Your "perception" will be found attractive by those potential clients, advocates, or job leads who relate very closely to it. They can identify with it, because they too have a similar perception of themselves. People like to work with others of like mind, with whom they are comfortable. Don't be offended if the signals that you send to potential clients, advocates, etc., are not well received from your perspective. They just may not be a "good match" for you and your talents. Remember, everyone is different. And, you cannot be everything to everyone.

Clearly, you would consider wearing different clothing to an interview with a large corporate client than to one with a residential customer who seeks a home addition. Residential customers may be overwhelmed by a "corporate image" suit and may feel that they cannot afford your services or are too small for your firm. Of course, your company may not have the opportunity to work in both arenas. However, when opportunity knocks, you must seize it!

The fact of the matter is that your image will change throughout the life of the firm. So start out striving for a strong, realistic, obtainable image. The reality is, if you are a sole proprietor and attempt to market yourself as a large firm, a savvy client will probably not retain your services because you lack depth. If you were trained in a large firm with a specialty, say, in healthcare, focus on the smaller healthcare projects within hospitals, outpatient clinics, and physicians' offices. Your former employer's clients are contacts, and they may be willing to commission you to do smaller projects as a way of limiting their risk. At the same time, they will obtain good value, because the large firm may be more expensive and not put its "first string" designers on the small project.

Most important, make sure your firm's image is consistent with who you are, your values, and what you are all about. Potential clients can see through a false image or an image with which you are uncomfortable. For example, if a potential project involves designing a church and you have never worked on one—or taken the time to talk to designers who have, or researched the topic—you will probably not project authority, confidence, expertise, and competence. The odds for your selection will be thin.

When you develop the correct image—whether alone, with your partner(s), or with a marketing consultant—get comfortable with it, work with it, and refine it. You will find success much quicker.

SELECTING A NAME

Selecting your new firm's name is an important decision from an image, vision, and legal perspective. It is essential to be aware of the implications of selecting your name and to make it work from the outset. As a design professional, you sell yourself and your ideas. Your firm's name should promote you. The image that you create for your firm begins with its name, how it looks when written, how it works graphically with a logo, and how it sounds over the telephone. Choose a name that will serve you well for an indefinite period of time.

For many designers, their dream or vision has been "hanging a shingle" with their name on it. They want to let their creativity and imagination take charge. It is that simple! But before you do that, consider that a business name should be selected with care as well:

- Choose a name that is both pleasant and easy to pronounce.

- Choose a name that describes what you do. Compare:

  - Franklin & Associates, Inc., versus

  - Franklin & Associates, Architects, versus

  - FAI

- ◆ Do not select a name that will be limiting unless you understand and accept the limitations. Compare:

  - ● Kolscher Bridge Engineers versus Kolscher Engineering Group

  - ● Lavin Residential Interiors versus Lavin Interiors United

Your firm's name will have an emotional impact on all who hear and read it. For example, if you decide to incorporate your name, George Apple, into George Apple AIA, Architect, most who encounter the name will assume that you are a sole proprietor with few or no employees. For many designers, this is what they are comfortable with, and what they desire.

If you want to project a larger, more established, or different image to the world, consider one of the following:

The Office of George M. Apple AIA, Architect
Apple + Company, Architects
George Macintosh Apple and Associates, Architects
Apple Architects, Inc.
Apple Architecture, Inc.
Apple + Associates, Architects
GMA Architects

What's in a name? Be careful of fictitious names or names that need an explanation to every client. Some clients feel that if you use a fictitious name, you are hiding behind it. To most, however, the name doesn't matter, because they have contacted *you* and want *you* and *your firm* to design the project.

Remember, every time you change your company's name, you must change letterhead, business cards, telephone listings, signs, title blocks, office forms—the list goes on and on, and so do the associated costs! Apple & Associates will allow the inclusion of additional professionals, associates, and partners more easily than will George Apple, Architect. The term "& Associates" projects an awareness of others—and their relative importance in the company—to the world as well as to employees.

Finally, whatever name you choose, especially if you incorporate, check with the secretary of state in your area to make sure that you do not infringe upon another company's name.

SERVICE OFFERINGS

When you start your own firm, you need to organize your thoughts on what services you will be providing. This is not only for your benefit, but also for that of your clientele! I know it sounds so fundamental, but it is extremely valuable to document what services your firm can provide. Defining them will give you a better understanding of those service offerings that you will not be producing and will have to retain from consultants.

Your service offerings aren't just limited to the name of your profession! Much of the client public doesn't understand precisely what architecture, engineering, or interior design is. If you told one hundred people that you were an interior designer, you would probably get one hundred different reactions: "You select colors and furniture, right? You select fabrics? You program spatial needs?"

If you intend to provide services for different markets, you may want to have different lists of services for each market. You may, for example, feel qualified to perform master planning services for religious facilities but not for hospitals. Take the time to evaluate what your strengths are for each market that you can provide services for, and make a list for your benefit as well as for your potential clients. Chart 10 summarizes typical service offerings for a design firm.

CHART 10
Typical Design Service Offerings

Facilities Management
Inventory existing space allocations
Field survey existing space and equipment
CADD documentation of existing facilities
Master plan development

Interior Design
Programming
Space planning
Interior finish selection

Furniture specification
Existing furniture inventory

Architecture
Feasibility studies
Design
Historic preservation
Construction documents
Bid/negotiation phase services
Construction administration
In-house cost estimating
Expert testimony
Post-occupancy services

Engineering
Feasibility studies
Design
Construction documents
Bid/negotiation phase services
Construction administration
In-house cost estimating
Value engineering
Forensic engineering
Energy consulting

CADD Systems
Autocad
Intergraph

Planning
Programming
Master planning development
Feasibility studies

NICHE MARKETS

What are niche markets? When designers specialize by project type, some develop very profitable specialties, or niches. All designers have strengths and weaknesses. As a new firm owner, you need to capitalize on your strengths. If your background is in residential design, you need to hone your strengths and develop a niche in the residential market in your area.

To analyze your strengths or competencies, evaluate yourself in the following categories:

Design
Service
Technical competency
Delivery capability
Project cost knowledge
Schedule requirements
Fees

If you feel that you master all of the above in a particular market segment, then establish that segment as a niche—and market, market, market! Develop a vision and image for that niche. Develop a marketing plan that addresses the niche. Market your niche indirectly; and sell your background and service capabilities to direct-market opportunities.

WHERE ARE THE OPPORTUNITIES?

You're ready to rock and roll. You understand the difference between direct and indirect marketing. You've decided on the name of your firm. You have your image in mind. You determined who will conduct direct marketing. And you've developed the list of services you will offer.

So the next question is: Where are the opportunities and how do you make those opportunities happen?

Opportunities are all around. It is just a matter of recognizing that they are everywhere and that they sometimes come out of nowhere. As was mentioned previously about indirect marketing, the most important thing to remember in creating opportunities is that everyone you meet socially or professionally is a potential prospect, lead, or referral. That's not to say that you cultivate and manipulate these friends, associates, and acquaintances for what you can get out of them, but it does pay off to gather and maintain as many contacts as possible. Developing a good list of solid contacts is the beginning to turning opportunities into projects.

Past and present clients should be at the top of that list. Depending on the arrangement you may have with your former (or soon to be former) employer, as some require past employees to sign a noncompete agreement that prevents doing business with their clients, former clients are a great source of opportunity. They know how you work and you know what they want. And, if they are a one-time–project client or a noncompete client, they can still play an important role in your success by providing rec-ommendations, introductions, and/or references.

But, again, be sure there is no conflict in contacting these prospects.

If you are unable to contact past clients, you can directly market to those working for or around that client and project. Vendors, contractors, and con-sultants serve as outstanding avenues of information to potential project leads and as a source of referral. They are often the first—particularly vendors—to know what is going on behind the scenes in projects being developed. Project committee members are another excellent choice as contacts for the same reasons mentioned above: they know you and you know what they want. And, if they volunteered to help on that past project, they most likely will gladly vol-unteer any information they can to help you with your new venture, as well.

An often overlooked—but significant—source for making contacts is through family and friends. The string of acquaintances there can be endless. You never know whom your sister-in-law's uncle or your brother's wife's stepmother knows. Plus, introducing yourself to a contact as being part of the family or a close friend becomes an immediate good recommendation. Talking about your plans and aspirations with your family and friends, and asking directly if they know anyone who could be a resource for information, can add multiple contact opportunities to your list.

Major corporations and organizations, such as nonprofits and schools sys-tems, absolutely must be on your contact list. These large operations are always in need of a variety of services. No matter what they produce, there is a potential need for what you offer. But you have to be on their list of qual-ified vendors. And it's also relatively easy to be on their list. With one phone call you can arrange to have paperwork sent to you, or, better still, you could submit an application online. If it is unclear where to apply, look or ask for the purchasing or financial departments. Some operations may also have a construction or engineering department that requires services, too. The object is to get on as many lists as you can and, once there, to *stay* on those lists when updates and renewals are requested.

Have you ever thought of how your business and personal services consultants—accountant, banker, insurance agent—grow their businesses? They often do it through their customers' referrals and recommendations. Some may even rely solely on this technique. So why not use their methods yourself? They are another good source for your list. These professionals are in the business of making contacts and developing more business. You've probably already shared your plans and ambitions with them, so they have insight into your firm's goals. Take it another step further by asking if they can recommend contacts or if they know anyone on your lists above. Their contacts may be the most productive of all.

Last, but most important of all, get yourself out there! Network with groups and associations in your target and specialty markets; get involved with a local charity, volunteer with your kids' school programs, or join a neighborhood sports team. Get "your face in the place" and introduce yourself to everyone. Take your business cards (everywhere), offer a good strong handshake, and be interested in everything and everybody. Ask questions, listen attentively, and talk more about the other person than about yourself. Your goal is to be viewed as someone who listens, is knowledgeable, and enjoys getting to know people. Your internal goal is to have more people know who you are and to add those people (with referrals, recommendations, and project opportunities) as contacts to your list.

Remember, no matter the size of the town, city, or area, everyone is connected somehow. To make those connections work for you, you need to make as many contacts as possible. The more contacts you make, the greater the possibilities to increase your opportunities.

PROMOTIONAL MATERIALS

So you've begun to make contacts and your efforts are bringing in results. Prospects are interested in your firm. They want to know more about you, your services, and your experience. So now what do you do? You send them some promotional materials.

As part of your direct marketing, promotional materials encompass a variety of pieces with elements of written text and graphics. They can be designed to be a coordinated message or individually to address specific target market interests. Pamphlets, cover letters, résumés, project sheets or listings, and endorsement letters are just a sampling of materials to use. Still other pieces include organization charts, Web sites, and written articles.

Full, pre-printed, bound brochures are another form of marketing material, but for starting up your firm I recommend the above methods. There's no need to go to great expense in order to get your message across and to present your capabilities well. With the selection of computer graphics software and color printers available today, anyone can create a professional-looking promotional piece for very little investment. In starting out, it is best to be practical with your marketing dollars.

It is also vital to keep in mind that promotional materials do not have to be extravagant, large, or bound. They don't need to be epistles or great collections of information about you, your past projects, and what you want from the prospect. Something as visually simple as one page printed in black and white can make a dramatic impact.

The point, no matter what form you use for your promotional materials, is to communicate the message you want known about you and your firm. Content is still the most effective part of any piece. Be sure to convey who you are, the experience you provide, and what you can offer the recipient. And, again, don't be wordy or ramble in your writing. Be brief and to the point. As is often said, less is more; and this is particularly true when promoting yourself.

Cover Letter

The first piece in your store of materials is the cover letter. The cover letter serves to introduce (or reintroduce) your firm, summarize your capabilities, outline the enclosed supporting promotional materials, and ask for the opportunity to meet or be considered. In order for the reader to get your message quickly, one page is sufficient to demonstrate your experience, your market or design specialty (or specialties), and your interest in serving the prospect.

A list or sentence stating projects' names as examples of your work is a must. Choose projects that may be readily recognized by the reader. "Name dropping" clients is another effective way to make a good impression. Again, the goal in outlining projects and name dropping clients is for instant recognition and to raise the reader's opinion of you and peak his or her interest in your abilities.

References can also be offered in the letter, but be sure to contact those references first for permission to use their name and phone number or e-mail. All of your good work in producing an attention-grabbing cover letter can be ruined with one phone call to a reference who doesn't want to be bothered.

Bold or italic highlighting and "bullet" markers improve the readability of your letter and stand out from the paragraph text. These enhancements should be used for the major points you wish to convey. But deciding which point(s) to enhance and where can be tricky since you may believe everything in your letter is important for the reader to know. Be selective. Too many enhancements will be distracting and can take away from the letter's overall appearance. As in all promotional pieces, you always want the content to stand out most.

Have you ever read a letter that begins "I am writing this letter to . . ." and thought, "Well, duh, I know you are 'writing this letter' because I am *reading* it!"? Bland introductory statements work against your message. You want to seize attention and move the reader to continue. And the beginning of your letter is the perfect place to show that you will be brief and to the point.

Depending on whether—or how well—you know the recipient, your letter can open with thanking them for their time in reviewing your work, name dropping an acquaintance who recommended you make contact, or asking directly for consideration for a particular project.

Résumé

Your résumé is another key element in your promotional materials package. The résumé provides information of not only your education and employment backgrounds (more name recognition opportunities), but can list your participation in professional and civic interests. These non–work-related activities give the reader a closer look into who you are and what matters to you.

Résumés are rarely read top to bottom, so go ahead and use bullets, lists, and highlights to the maximum. One page is all you will need. Anything more than that could be considered bragging. And you want to save that for the other promotional pieces.

Project Examples

I don't need to tell you that examples of your work are essential. In fact, your inventory of projects may be the first piece (after glancing over your cover letter, of course) the reader looks for in your marketing package. Projects may be displayed as a listing or with a single project per page, depending on the number of projects you have to show and the information you have about each.

For those projects you want to demonstrate your best efforts and talents, use a single page with a description, client information (address, phone, and/or e-mail) as a reference, and, if possible, a visual of the work. In the description, be sure to include numbers such as square footage, wattage, acreage, cost, and dimension. This enables the reader to better visualize the size of the project *and* your capabilities.

Getting into the how's and what's of visuals is a subject best left to other authors, but some tips I think are important in getting you started in the right direction with your marketing materials are:

- ◆ Visuals are more than photographs, hand sketches, or computer renderings. The means to present your work are limitless.

- ◆ Visuals don't have to be high-end, but they do have to show the overall effect of the project and the design elements.

- ◆ If you do your own photography, look closely at the scene to determine what may negatively stand out, such as signage, dust and dirt, background distractions, or shadow. These diminish the general impact of the image and may possibly be what the viewer sees first, or only.

- ◆ Don't make the images too small. It may be "artsy" to have multiple small visuals, but you took the time and spent the money to create them, so make sure they are printed large enough to see. The outcome of your work could be lost if the details aren't visible.

Packaging Your Promotional Materials

How you assemble or "package" your promotional materials or even how that packaging looks is not the deal breaker of whether or not you make a good initial impression. (I've seen marketing packages that are relatively plain on the outside, but the inside content knocks my socks off.) But, yes, it is significant. There are several options to packaging: pocket folders, spiral or ring bindings, and loose-leaf binders. Or you can also just paperclip your materials together in a large envelope. No matter what you decide to use, keep in mind the purpose of packaging is for the recipient to be able to keep your materials together in one location on a desk, on a shelf, or in a file drawer for easy reference and retrieval.

Getting Help

Although it is possible to create your own promotional pieces with today's vast array of graphics software, pre-printed papers, and store-bought packaging, I do recommend seeking assistance from a graphics college student or moon-lighting graphics professional in laying out your project sheets and résumés. As a designer, you know how you want your promotional materials to look. But as an entrepreneur, you don't have time to sit in front of the computer for hours that are better spent completing a project or marketing a prospect. Hiring help gives you the time to do it all, and do it well.

And one last recommendation before you go off to create remarkable promotional materials that launch your firm to success: Engage the skills of a teacher, English graduate student, or journalist. Have them write or, at a minimum, review the text of your marketing pieces. Not to offend anyone, but designers (including myself) are not particularly known for their grammar, punctuation, and writing skills. In fact, several individuals evaluated, rewrote, edited, and condensed this book to make it more legible for you.

Once you have the direct-market lead and offer your service capabilities, the potential client, feeling comfortable with your background and firm, will probably ask for a proposal for professional services. One-third of the battle is won by getting in the door; the next third is to convince the client in person and in writing that you can solve the particular problems involved. This is referred to in the business world as "sales." (The final third, of course, is getting the job done!) Be aggressive and proactive in marketing the services of your firm.

WRITING A PROPOSAL THAT SELLS

The formal way to sell your capabilities and services is through a written proposal. Proposal writing is an art. There are as many opinions on writing proposals as there are ways to write them. Remember, always personalize your proposals. Customize each one. Tell clients what you understand or perceive to be their need, and how you plan to solve their challenges and satisfy their needs. Be careful to express yourself clearly regarding what services you feel each client needs, as well as those that you feel the client does not need. Proposals that are direct, to the point, and written in simple, understandable language will be appreciated and will help sell your firm because you will exhibit accountability and responsibility to your potential client. Your client will develop trust in your firm because your actions demonstrate care and concern. The best compliment in sales is to receive a compliment that "Your proposal was the most understandable, concise, organized, easy-to-follow proposal of the five that we received. *Thank you for making our job of reviewing the proposal easy. Our impression of your firm is that you are well-organized, you listened, you understand our need, and, although your proposed fee is higher than the others, we are not confident that they perceive our needs as well as you do.*"

Write your proposal following the format shown in chart 11. It will give you and your client as close to a comprehensive document as possible. Before you begin, be sure to examine the sample proposal shown in appendix A.

When you summarize your scope of services, use chart 12 as a guide. It is a comprehensive checklist of design service tasks that are normally offered to clients. The list is generic since there are no longer any "standard" or "normal" services on a design project.

. . . .
Your firm's policy is that it cannot begin work on the project without an executed (signed) proposal.
. . . .

Enforce this rule for yourself and all your clients. At best, potential problem clients will recognize that you are business-oriented and will treat you accordingly. Also, some clients may warrant a formal contract. A signed proposal will allow you to begin work; you can then develop a formal contract to be executed before the design of the project is completed.

If there is one fundamental mistake that designers make more than others it is in proposal/contract preparation. Be concise, firm, and definitive. Most important, write the proposal and get it executed!

. . . .
Always request down payments in your proposals.
. . . .

CHART 11
Typical Proposal Format

I. SCOPE OF WORK
Summarize what the client has told you and what the client expects of you. Be explicit and complete. There are never enough words to describe a client's expectations. Then tell the client how you plan to organize your capabilities into a scope of work. List the phases that are detailed below.

II. PHASES
Describe each phase, when and how it begins, what you will be doing, and what the product of the phase is. How many meetings will you have with the client? Define the time frame (schedule) and associated fee for each phase. Describe how the phase ends, and how it leads into the next phase.

III. SUMMARY OF FEES
Summarize all fees by phase and total the "bottom line."

IV. EXCLUSIONS
Tell the client what you specifically have not included in your scope of work. Be precise, and do not worry about using too many items or words. This may be the most important section of your proposal, because the client may recognize certain items not included in your scope of work (or in your fee) that he or she wants to include in the project.

V. ADDITIONAL SERVICES
Tell the client that anything not mentioned in the scope of work is excluded and considered an additional service. State that your firm will be delighted to take on additional services. You will quote the client a fee for each request based on your standard hourly rates. List your rates.

VI. REIMBURSABLE EXPENSES

It is important to differentiate between services and expenses. Tell the client that you will charge for automobile mileage, printing, photography, long-distance telephone communications, and other expenses associated with the project.

VII. MISCELLANEOUS PROVISIONS

This section reinforces certain points that are discussed in the other six sections. Here is where you make your proposal complete. Stress important issues such as payment terms, terms of the proposal effectiveness, interest on late payments, down payments, and your right to withhold drawings if the client has not paid. Most important, in your last paragraph describe how important the project is to you and how you look forward to working with the client.

VIII. ACCEPTANCE

Develop language that the client will acknowledge and sign to bind your services.

Another important "trip-wire" to catch "potentially bad" clients is requesting a down payment for your services. If a prospective client is not willing to commit an initial investment of a few dollars to "seal the deal" with you and your firm, they may be a client that will not pay you on time, or at all. Always ask for a down payment. All the prospective client can say is "no," and then you can make the decision on whether to continue or not with the project. Always apply the value of the down payment against the last invoice of the project. That way, you can use the value of the money up-front to help finance your needs to perform the work on the project. A down payment always helps cash flow. Think of it: If you start work without any fee up-front, you will do design work for at least thirty days, you will invoice the client after forty days, and you might receive payment after seventy days! Get some money up-front. You will be amazed how that will help your cash flow and profits. Also, if there is a dispute at the end of the project with the client, and they hold your last invoice for whatever reason, you already have the value of the down payment in your pocket that you would have deducted off of the last invoice, so you are that amount ahead of the client. A down payment leverages a lot for a firm through the design process.

CHART 12
Typical Design Service Tasks

Predesign Services
Project-related research
Predesign conferences
Development of fees and contracts
Reviewing owner data for the project
Procuring existing drawings of the site or building
Programming spatial requirements
Evaluating site requirements
Documentation of existing conditions
    Photography
    Field measurement
    Field verification services (not intensive measurement/
       confirmation of layout only)
    Drafting of existing conditions
Analysis of existing engineering capabilities
    Structural
    Mechanical/electrical/plumbing
Marketing studies
Feasibility studies
Preliminary project budgeting and scheduling
Presentations of any of the above

Site Analysis Services
Procuring necessary surface/subsurface site data
Procuring title information on property

- Procuring new survey data
- Site photography
- Agency/jurisdiction review and approval process
- Zoning process services
- Community organization review and approval process
- Environmental group review and approval process
- Site analysis
- Site development planning
- Site utility studies
- Environmental studies and delineation
- Project budgeting and scheduling
- Presentation of any of the above

Conceptual Design Services
- Conceptual design sketches
- Study models
- Perspective sketches
- Computer animations
- Conceptual engineering design requirements
- Agency/jurisdiction review
- Project budgeting and scheduling
- Presentation of any of the above
- Owner approval process

Design Refinement (Development) Services
- Refined plans of conceptual design
- Refined elevations, sections, details of conceptual design
- Engineering design refinement drawings
- Outline specification of material selections
- Study model(s)
- Refined perspective sketches
- Computer animations
- Agency/jurisdiction review
- Estimate of probable construction costs
- Project scheduling

Presentation of any of the above
Owner approval process

Construction Document/Permit Document Services

Development of documentation for construction and permit application
Engineering documentation for construction and permit application
Specifications for material selections
Final models
Final computer animations
Professional renderings
Agency/jurisdiction review
Estimate of probable construction costs
Project scheduling
Presentation of any of the above
Owner approval process

Bid/Negotiation Phase Services

Compilation of bidding material
Identification and procurement of bidders
Prequalification of bidders
Prebid meetings
Coordination and answering questions during bid phase
Development of addenda for clarifications
Procuring bids
Attending bid opening
Evaluation of bids
Assisting owner in awarding contract
Participation in negotiations
Assisting owner in notifying all bidders of results
Assisting owner in developing notice to proceed

Construction Phase Services

Office services
    Review of submittals
    Telephone coordination

       Coordination of change order requests

       Interpreting intent of documents

       Preparing clarification drawings

       Project schedule monitoring

       Procurement of all releases of liens

       Issuance of certificate of substantial completion

       Record documentation/maintenance manuals

       Issuance of final approval for payment to contractor

On-site services

       Review of progress

       Review of contractor's payment requests

       Punch list documentation

       Final walk-through

Special Services

Special studies

Renderings

Life-cycle cost analysis

Value architecture/engineering analysis

Professional cost estimating services

Environmental/energy analysis

Graphic design

Project marketing artwork development

Expert witness testimony

Special engineering consultant coordination services

Any service not listed above pertinent to design

SELLING

Selling is different from marketing. Selling is part of marketing.

Selling is promoting yourself and your talents to potential clients. Selling is convincing clients that you can help them solve their challenges. You must sell the importance of human chemistry, reliability, service, design, accountability, and genuine care for the client. Selling is not sending out a form letter or advertising in a magazine.

Once you have done your job of indirect marketing, you will have leads to begin your direct-marketing phase. The potential client has asked for a proposal from your firm—as well as from three other firms! How is the client going to make a decision?

In the sales world, those qualities that make your firm unique are referred to as "differentiators." How are we different from our competition? How will these differences make us a better choice to select for the prospect? You don't want to be perceived the same as the competition. Your competition is other designers, but what makes you different? Unique? Desirable in being considered and selected?

Even before you develop your proposal, you need to ask the client a few questions to help you demonstrate that you are overwhelmingly interested in the project and that you care for the client's needs. The answers that you receive will tell you a lot about the project, the client, and your chances of being commissioned to do the work! Tailor your proposal around the client's answers to the following questions—to separate your firm from the rest of the pack (the competition):

What do you have in mind for the project?

What are your needs for the project?

Is anyone against the project?

What is the funding source for the project?

If my firm is selected, with whom will it be in contract and to whom will it be accountable?

Is a committee involved in the presentation process? Who are the members of the committee, and what do they do for a living?

Who makes the decision on awarding the contract?

Have you or your organization ever worked with a design professional before? Who?

Who are the other design professionals my firm is competing with?

What kind of fee structure do you have in mind?

What is your estimated budget for the project?

After the presentations and proposals are made, how long will it take to award the contract?

While you are direct marketing for the potential project, you also need to ask your client about the criteria for selecting a design professional. The following list incorporates most of the criteria clients use in comparing designers:

Does the designer understand the project?
Does the designer understand my/our needs?
Does the designer have the experience/background to perform?
How long will it take the designer to perform the services?
How much will it cost?

Once you determine the criteria for selection, address them in your proposal! Identify the client's "hot buttons" in boldface or italics. Show the client that you care. Listen and take the time to effectively communicate how you will address the client's needs better than the competition! This is selling.

Clients will review your proposal as well as submissions from the competition and will develop certain perceptions about each competitor.

Clients will probably compare your firm with competitors on the following points:

Is the firm large or small, and can its size meet our expectations for the project?
Is the firm local or out of town, and can its location meet our expectations?
Is the firm an expert or a novice in this project type?

Many clients select the designer who "wants to design our project the most"! Other clients base their selection primarily on price. Still others want "name" firms only and are simply shopping the project, asking your firm (and others) for a proposal to use as a negotiating tool with the "name" firm. Determine early in the direct-marketing stage what type of potential client you have.

What you should hope for is a client that selects the successful firm based upon its qualifications and proposal, and that the client believes that the culture of the design firm is a "good match" for the client's entity.

PRESENTATIONS

After you have done your indirect and direct marketing, find out the type of potential client you have and write a proposal. You may be asked to make a presentation or meet with the client to explain your proposal and answer questions.

When you meet face to face with your potential client, remember that selling with smooth words and hot phrases is one thing. Substance is another. When you deliver the presentation, do it with enthusiasm, confidence, authority, professionalism, and above all commitment to the project! Every client is different, and will react differently to certain selling techniques. You must tailor each and every presentation to that particular client.

Many designers have found out the hard way that lengthy presentations of their work—a staple of the past—have become boring to the prospective client as a sales technique. Clients obviously want to know about you and your firm's experience; but their major concern is how you are going to help them. They want to meet you, see you, and encounter and observe your mannerisms and body language during the interview. When you darken the lights and show PowerPoint slide after slide of your work, the presentation becomes a "one way street" with very little interaction and dialogue. If you must show presentation slides, keep them to a minimum. Strategically place a few visuals in your presentation as "teasers" to entertain the client.

Your selling skills will improve with experience and over time. Be patient. You will make plenty of mistakes. Many a designer has spent enormous amounts of time in indirect and direct marketing only to "blow it" when it came to selling the job. The most important thing you can do in this case is to attempt to get debriefed by the client. Get the client's impression of the presentation, and learn from it. You never know when that client will give you a chance again in the future. The next time, you will be a little more savvy, experienced, and prepared. Remember, be genuine, be yourself, be comfortable, be appreciative for the opportunity, and most importantly, convey that your experience will allow you to assist this client like no one else will. Selling takes practice, practice, and more practice!

MARKETING IS A WAY OF LIFE

The marketing process starts with the perceived image and ends with the sale of the contract.

Thus, when you market yourself and your firm, you must carefully calculate the image that you want to create. You and your marketing efforts must project authority, confidence, friendliness, accountability, responsibility, vision, and leadership.

Marketing is not selling. Selling is only a part of marketing! Selling is getting a client to agree to hire you and your firm. Remember, your vision in indirect marketing, direct marketing, and selling is to get the client to say yes. Structure your selling strategy so that you are comfortable with your offering to the client. Effectively say what you will do, and then back it up by doing what you say. Finally, write an effective proposal that communicates your care and understanding for the client's challenges and needs. Get their attention. Get the interview, and be genuine and yourself.

Continue this process/cycle over and over again. From it, you will gain experience, respect, and a name. A solid, quality reputation is one of the major selling tools that a firm can have.

8

LEGAL CONSIDERATIONS

"People do not win people fights. Lawyers do."
—NORMAN R. AUGUSTINE

"If the present Congress errs in too much talking, how can it be otherwise in a body to which the people send one hundred and fifty lawyers, whose trade it is to question everything, yield nothing, and talk by the hour?"
—THOMAS JEFFERSON

Can I afford to retain a lawyer? Lawyers are so expensive! Maybe I can go to the library and read up on the legal issues and do it myself. Why do I need a lawyer? Why can't I just practice architecture, and not worry about legal issues? Why must I be so organized, or appear that way?

I'll call a lawyer when I really need one.

Partnership agreements, buy-sell agreements, articles of incorporation—why is business so complicated? All I want to do is design! No one told me about all this legal jazz.

I wonder if I should have an attorney review this contract?

Looks like I may have a liability claim. Is it too late to contact a lawyer?

DO I NEED A LAWYER TO HELP START MY FIRM?

There is a very simple answer to this question: yes.

Every business decision has legal implications: dealing with money and taxes, writing contracts and proposals, conducting all correspondence, hiring staff, setting your fee structure, signing and sealing your drawings, paying your bills, etc. The fatality rate of small businesses is enormously high. The odds are about 10:1 that your firm will fail in the first three years of its existence! Therefore, it is extremely important that you establish a sound legal foundation for the new firm. However, as discussed in previous chapters, keep your organization simple. You do not have to hire legal corporate counsel that has a worldwide reputation. The simplest thing to do is to speak with one of your colleagues, call your local design association (AIA, ASID, NSPE) component office, or talk with the legal counsel from the firm that you last worked for. Call and ask for an attorney who has experience with business start-ups. Ask the individual if he or she will "sell you" one to two hours of his or her time for a "Business Start-up Legal 101" class. Spending $400–$500 for this time will be well worth it. You need to find out about business forms and, most importantly, what business laws are and how businesses operate in your state. If you are an architect, review the architect's law of your state with the attorney, and do the same if you are an engineer or interior designer. You are required to know what is expected of you. If you find the correct attorney, she not only will help you with the "101" course but will check in from time to time to see how you are doing. Attorneys will tell you that ignorance is no excuse for not knowing business law or the designer's law in your state. As a business owner, you are expected to know the law because you deal with the public and are commended with their trust.

Types of Legal Counsel

There are two types of lawyers that you will need to help you start your firm. (Some designers are fortunate to find a lawyer who can assume both roles.) First, you need a lawyer who understands small business, whose practice is centered around it. Such lawyers genuinely care about their small business clients; they have the same attitude toward the health of a fledgling firm as a physician has toward the health of a patient. This kind of legal counsel will help you decide what form of business to establish and will process the necessary paperwork with the local jurisdiction.

The second kind of lawyer you will need is one who understands contract law, especially construction law and professional design agreements. If you are an architect, the *American Institute of Architects' Handbook on Professional Practice* has just about all the contract forms you will ever need. Still, it is advisable to retain counsel to review any special contracts or hybrids that may be prepared by your clients.

Remember, attorneys are like architects, engineers, and interior designers. Most have specialties or niches of practice. Some concentrate in divorce law, others in bodily injury cases, others in real estate, and some in business law, let alone design laws. Having a "divorce specialist" may not be the right match for your needs as a start-up firm. Be honest with yourself. Don't select an attorney just because she is an acquaintance or offers a reasonable fee structure for services.

Retaining the services of counsel to discuss the many legal pitfalls of starting a new firm is a form of self-protection. All of us have felt the temptation to save money on legal fees in the beginning by purchasing guidebooks and looking for "free" advice. This is the worst thing we could do; we are trained as designers, not lawyers.

Selecting a Lawyer

How well you select your lawyer will have a direct impact on your firm's success. You should meet with at least three candidates before you make your selection. How do you get the names of three lawyers or firms? One of the most reliable methods is to get personal recommendations from your banker, from friends or colleagues, or from your local AIA/CEC/ASID office. Make sure that you interview lawyers who understand designers and the practice of design in your state. Make sure that your attorney has the proper credentials or professional designation (LLB or JD). Remember, though, that credentials and certification ensure only that an attorney has the minimum standard of education. There are no guarantees that the individual will be a creative business adviser with the necessary experience to fit your needs.

Fees will vary by the size of the firm and the experience of the lawyer. Firms with low rates may be concerned with high volume and not give you the attention that your new enterprise requires. High hourly rates tend to be associated with more conservative, less aggressive firms that are reluctant to spend time with small business clients, since their priorities rest with larger corporations. The lawyers in the middle fee range are the ones you should look for. They are in demand, however, because they are generally aggressive and innovative. Also, they care about small business—which accounts for 80 percent of business in the United States. It is important to be very open and discuss the lawyer's hourly rates, and what you will be getting for them. Most attorneys work "on retainer," which means that you pay a fee allowance up front that will provide up to so many hours per month, quarter, or year for their services. You can call or meet with them at will, billing against the time allotted for the retainer. When you exhaust your time or fee retainer, you normally enter into another arrangement. Attorneys do not like to invoice for fractions of hours on a monthly basis. They would rather have your money up front, and then charge against it over time based on your needs and use.

Finally, select a lawyer whom you are most comfortable with and, most important, whom you will trust. It is so important to work with legal counsel who has experience and tells stories about other designers and their challenges, and what he or she learned from them. This knowledge and understanding of the design business is priceless. If you are represented by a respected, experienced attorney in your field of design, should the time come when you need him or her to defend your firm and its interests, the other parties in the action may look at you differently. You always hope that your prospective clients think you are the best choice to design their project, and you expect them to be proud of your design and refer you to others. You should feel the same way about your legal counsel.

FORMS OF BUSINESS

Now that you have selected an attorney and are ready to set up your new firm, you need to understand what forms of business exist and which form is right for you. There are several forms of business for a start-up firm to consider: sole proprietorship, partnership, a regular corporation and Subchapter S corporation, and Limited Liability Partnerships and Limited Liability Corporations. Verify with your attorney which forms are permissible in your state of practice. As your business grows in the future, and you become licensed in other states, it is quite possible that you could operate two or more business forms, based on the requirements of the various state laws.

Sole Proprietorship

A sole proprietorship is the simplest form of business. The company is you and you are the company. In many cases, the only legality of this form of business is filing the appropriate tax returns. You must pay a quarterly estimate of your income tax and social security (self-employment tax), and you must retain all records of the business's transactions.

The following are advantages of starting as a sole proprietorship:

Ease of formation
Low cost of registration and legal expense
Lack of complexity
Simple decision-making process
Sole ownership of profits
Ease of termination or sale of the firm
Flexibility

The following are disadvantages:

Unlimited personal liability
Less financing capacity with lenders (banks)
Unstable duration of the business owing to owner's illness or death
Sole decision-making
Taxation on profits at certain levels
Limited business deductions

Unlimited liability is no doubt the biggest disadvantage. Many sole proprietors transfer title of their personal assets to their spouses to protect themselves from business liabilities! Another major disadvantage is that banks doubt the stability of sole proprietorships, since their success rests on one key individual. Finally, unlike corporations, sole proprietors may have tax challenges in taking the costs of automobiles, health insurance, and charitable contributions as business deductions. You need to verify all aspects of the business law in your state about this form of business before you commit to it.

Partnership

A partnership is a written or oral agreement between two or more parties to carry on a business. In a partnership, each partner contributes capital, services, and assets to share in the business's profit or loss.

An important issue in a partnership is that each partner is subject to unlimited personal liability for the debts of the partnership. Also, each partner is liable for the negligence of another partner and of the partnership's employees! Therefore, before you enter into a partnership, there are two concerns you should address:

1. If I go into partnership with _____, is this a responsible, accountable person for whom I am going to be liable?

2. Can I get enough insurance to adequately insure and protect the partnership, as well as my personal assets and my partner's?

As you can see, a partnership is significantly more complex than a sole proprietorship, although most states do not require any formalities of documentation. If your partnership does not have a formal "partnership agreement," your state law will determine the terms. State laws in general are based on fundamental characteristics of the partnership as it has existed throughout time. Here are the most important of the legally presumed characteristics:

- No one can enter into a partnership without the consent and approval of all partners.

- All partners have an equal vote in the operations of the partnership.

- A simple majority vote is required for ordinary business decisions, and a unanimous vote is required to change the fundamental characteristics of the partnership.

- All partners share equally in the profits and losses of the partnership.

- A partner can withdraw from the business at any time, causing the partnership to dissolve.

These are just a few basics. Each state will have different presumed characteristics. Therefore, since each partnership is different simply because the individuals involved are different, it is highly recommended that you employ legal counsel to help you draft a formal partnership agreement that recognizes your special requirements for a new design firm.

The major considerations that go into a partnership agreement include:

Name of the partnership	Sale of partnership interest
Description of the business	Additions and modifications
Capital contributions made	to the partnership agreement
by each partner	Noncompetition agreements
Duration of the partnership	in the event of a partner's
Nature and degree of each	departure
partner's contribution	Method of distributing
Business expenses and how	profits
they will be handled	Management responsibilities
Separate debts	(marketing/administration/
Signing of checks	design/production/
Draws or salaries	construction administration)
Absence and disability	Duties of partners
Death of a partner and rights	Prohibited acts
of continuing partners	Dissolution of the partnership

Given the complexities and potential problems involved in a partnership, it is surprising that so many designers operate without partnership agreements! Most just want to design, not spend time on the important details of the business organization. However, because of the nature of a partnership, it is essential to have an agreement.

The benefits and disadvantages of a partnership are similar to those of a sole proprietorship. Partnerships can be easy to form and "require" minimal paperwork. The greatest disadvantage is the potential conflict among the partners. Personal disagreements over the firm's operation or design approaches will hurt the business.

Business relationships often lead to good friendships, but friendships rarely survive a business relationship.

Nowhere is this truer than in a partnership.

The advantages of forming a partnership are:

Ease of formation
Pride of ownership

Direct rewards of profit (since more people are involved)
Greater availability of capital
Combination of expertise and talent
Flexibility
Relative freedom from government control and special taxation

The disadvantages are:

Unlimited liability
Conflict over terms of partnership agreement
Unstable duration of agreement
Management difficulties
Difficulty in obtaining large sums of capital from lenders (banks)
Difficulty of disposing of partnership interest

Corporation

A corporation is a legal entity that can be established by one or more individuals or legal entities. Its existence is separate and distinct from the individuals or other legal entities. The most important difference between a corporation and a partnership is the fact that the owners of the corporation (shareholders or stockholders) are not personally liable for the corporation's debts. For a small professional design corporation, however, this limited liability may be an illusion, since lenders often require owners to personally cosign for any credit or loans. In addition, designers are personally responsible for their own wrongful or negligent acts.

Many start-up owners are tempted to form a corporation immediately because it underscores their decision and lends prestige to their firm. The corporate form, however, can be complex and very expensive to create and dissolve. As a designer, you would do well to work as a sole proprietor for at least a year to make sure that you have your act together. Starting business as a sole proprietor costs very little, reducing your capital requirements and lowering your overhead. After a year of experience, you should then explore the option of incorporating with your accountant and attorney.

The following are advantages of forming a corporation:

Limited liability of shareholders
Flexibility for tax planning
Corporate management flexibility

Financing readily available

Continued existence of the corporation beyond death of a shareholder

Ownership readily transferable

Expertise available from more than one individual

The following are disadvantages:

Extensive government regulation

Activities limited by charter and bylaws

Majority shareholders can manipulate minority shareholders in voting

Expenses of incorporation process

Incorporating is generally a fairly simple matter, but to do it right the first time and to minimize costs and time, you should retain the services of an attorney. Since a lawyer's time is money, you can save both by using this checklist of points to discuss with your attorney:

Corporate name

Corporate structure

Names of officers

Names of shareholders

Shareholder agreements

Buy-sell agreement

Planning for future shareholders

Capitalization

Board of directors

Registered agent of the corporation (usually the incorporating
    attorney)

Most jurisdictions require "articles of incorporation" to be filed and approved before the corporation can conduct business. The articles summarize all of the above items.

Subchapter S (Sub-S) Corporation

If you elect the corporate form of business, you may wish to consider the advantages of a Sub-S corporation in the United States. Simply stated, the purpose of the Sub-S is to permit a small business corporation to treat its net income as though it were a partnership. This helps overcome the double taxation feature of the corporation, in which both corporate income and shareholder dividends are taxed. In addition, the Sub-S allows shareholders to offset business losses against their income. If a corporation anticipates losses during its first year or more, the Sub-S format may be desirable to minimize tax liabilities.

Again, this issue should be discussed with your accountant and lawyer, since Sub-S forms of incorporation are not recognized in all states.

Other Forms of Business

Other forms of business, such as Limited Liability Corporations or LLC's and Limited Liability Parnterships or LLP's, exist and have different requirements in the various state laws. Some states do not allow design firms to practice under the "Limited Liability" name due to the perception that the design professional has "limited his or her liability" in regards to the protection of the public's welfare and safety. Lawmakers make laws that make designers liable for what they design, to protect the interests of the general public. Verify the pros and cons of these business forms and how they fare in your state with your legal counsel.

Licensing of Your Partnership or Corporation

Be aware that many states require that, in addition to your personal license to practice your design discipline, you register your business entity to practice in the state. This form of registration occurs not only to raise revenues, but also to identify to the state what types of business you perform, and whether or not you need to charge sales tax on your services or products sold. This registration identifies your organization to the state tax and assessment departments and makes it subject to periodic audits for sales tax collection and other fees. If you have any doubts about this form of licensing, contact your state office of licensing and registration boards to acquire a copy of your state law, and discuss your needs with their staff.

KEEP IT SIMPLE

In the beginning, keep it simple. Work with your attorney to choose the form of business ownership that is right for you. As time and success grow your firm, you will need to investigate the various forms again to determine if a change is required due to liability, tax, or legal issues. Many firms change their form of business several times in their history. Knowing when to consider invoking a change in business form, as well as consulting with your firm's legal counsel, is your responsibility. This is one of the most important decisions that you will ever make. Do it right the first time to set a successful course in your business legal future. Embrace your responsibility for knowledge of the current business and legal issues that face your area's design discipline. Do not ignore them. Having knowledge will diminish your legal risks each and every day that you run your firm and practice.

9

INSURANCE CONSIDERATIONS

"Simply by not owning three medium-sized castles in Tuscany I have saved enough money in the last forty years on insurance premiums alone to buy a medium-sized castle in Tuscany."

—LUDWIG MIES VAN DER ROHE

"There are worse things in life than death. Have you ever spent an evening with an insurance salesman?"

—WOODY ALLEN

I hate insurance salespeople. They are worse than used car people! I avoid dealing with them.

Why do I need insurance? No one is going to sue me! I care too much about my clients and their projects.

Whole life versus term, whole life versus term. I've talked to three insurance agents, and am I ever confused!

I can't afford health insurance, so I hope my spouse keeps his job so that we retain coverage at his company.

I can't possibly afford liability insurance. I'll just have to go naked for a while, and keep my fingers crossed.

I don't own anything of value, personally, so let someone sue me.

DO I NEED INSURANCE WHEN I START MY FIRM?

Every new business venture represents a gamble, because it is difficult to predict the future. Even with adequate financing, a well-mapped business plan, and a backlog of projects to work on, the chances for success hover around the 50:50 mark at best! Business opportunities present a speculative risk that is two-directional: win or lose. As in gambling, you may lose sometimes and then you may win. Hopefully you will win more than you lose. Luck is a factor here, of course. However, there exist in life some one-directional risks—fire, death, disability—in which the outcome is always a loss. Such one-directional risks are called pure risks. Insurance exists primarily to protect individuals and companies against losses caused by pure risks that damage property, life, or limb.

Accidents happen, people sue, disasters strike unexpectedly. You can't live in fear, wondering if a truck will hit you when you cross the next street. However, the sign of a good businessperson is the willingness to protect a business. It is imperative that you not only accept the existence of pure risk, but also learn how to live with it and manage it. Proper risk management means planning for potential problems and attempting to insure against them. You must spend some time familiarizing yourself with the numerous types of insurance available on the market, and how to obtain them. Here are a few suggestions on developing your plan to protect your new firm from pure risks:

> 1. Think in terms of a well-planned program that starts out in a simple, affordable way, one that can grow with the business. As the firm grows, and you age, so will the risks. Therefore, don't buy too much insurance in the beginning. But how do you know what is too much?

> 2. Seek professional help at the outset. Designers are certainly not experts in risks and insurance. Again, as in choosing a lawyer, accountant, or banker, you need to find a professional broker who understands small businesses, especially design firms. Most important, you need an insurance broker who genuinely cares about you and the success of your firm. If, in your first meeting with this person, all you think about is how much insurance he or she is trying to sell you, you are with the wrong insurance broker. It may take time, but find a broker with whom you are comfortable, one who is approachable and easily accessible.

3. List your risk priorities. Insurance protection against a catastrophe should be near the top of the list (property and casualty). Insuring your new firm's premises against fire, earthquake, flood, etc. is very important. You cannot afford to lose your new firm's assets early on unless, of course, you are individually wealthy. Professional liability insurance is also a major priority. Insurance companies, over time, have focused on the small start-up firm's needs, and have attempted to create insurance coverage that is affordable for the new firms.

4. Hold down excessive costs by talking frankly with your broker, looking at several options in coverage, premiums, and deductibles. It is wise to investigate the advantages of package policies.

5. Keep accurate records of what your policies cover so that in the event of a claim, you will have a complete listing for the insurance company and thus will diminish your firm's downtime.

6. Modify your insurance policies to changing conditions in your firm. Every time you purchase an asset, make sure it is covered. As the company grows and becomes more valuable, make sure the insurance coverage grows with it.

Businesspeople and entrepreneurs are often reluctant even to discuss pure risk because it is a negative, pessimistic topic over which they have no control. How many people do you know with the attitude "I can't worry about things I can't control"? Also, many people dislike meeting with insurance agents—whom they rank just below used car sellers—because they do not understand the fine points of insurance and feel that they are always being taken advantage of.

The fact of the matter is that we can't constantly worry about disasters and things we can't control; but as businesspeople, as risk takers, we must implement plans to "hedge our bets."

This is another aspect of business that everyone expects to be addressed by the firm's leadership. Insurance is always a pain to pay for, but when you need it, thank heavens that you have it. If you don't, you may be faced with a challenge through which you can't succeed.

OBTAINING INSURANCE

Insurance companies market their services chiefly through agencies, brokers, and clubs and associations.

> 1. Agencies. Agencies are smaller, individualized operations that place home, car, and other common types of insurance with several insurance companies with whom they are affiliated. Since they must meet quotas with the different carriers, they may try to sell you policies that do not totally suit your needs or are not totally competitive.

> 2. Brokers. Brokers claim to have complete independence from any insurance company and offer more flexibility than any agency. Brokers usually have no vested interest in placing insurance with any particular company, and will therefore attempt to get you the best premiums and coverage to meet your needs. Talk to at least three brokers. If they are using the same insurance base for the best coverage and premiums, then all should recommend the same companies for the different forms of coverage you are requesting.

> 3. Clubs and associations. Contact your local Better Business Bureau, chamber of commerce, or AIA chapter about its group insurance rates.

TYPES OF INSURANCE

The types of insurance you will need will vary with your risks. The following overview of insurance coverage is provided to make you aware of what exists and the types of insurance that might be appropriate. If you already have coverage (life insurance, car insurance, etc.), meet with your present agents to discuss your plans for your new firm. If they have been trustworthy to date with your personal insurance needs, they should be able to help you with your simple, start-up business insurance needs. Remember, after you conduct your research, only you can make the final decision on which insurance to select and purchase. Don't feel pressured by your agent. Be confident that the decision you are making is a valid one, and that the insurance is not overpriced, is fair, and meets your coverage needs. Should something happen, this insurance should "make you whole," not reward you with a multiple of times your former value.

General Liability

A general liability policy covers losses due to bodily injury or damage to the property of others; all emergency, medical, and surgical expenses incurred from accidents; expenses to cover investigations; and your defense, settlement, and trial costs. The policy covers negligence causing injury to clients, employees, and the general public. It is normally written up as a comprehensive liability policy. This is necessary to obtain as close to day one of your start-up as possible.

Completed Operations Liability

This policy offers protection against a lawsuit by a client who used your services and as a result sustained bodily injury or property damage.

Professional Liability (Errors and Omissions Liability)

This coverage protects you and other design professionals on your consulting team against litigation arising from losses incurred by your clients as a result of a design error or omission and negligence. Make sure your broker shops this coverage. Premiums are based on your annual revenue volume and the type of projects that you design. If you are a start-up, your coverage will be based upon your projected revenue and project types. That is why it is important to not only know yourself, but also have vision to predict what projects you will design and the resultant estimated fees. You will document these ideas in your business and marketing plans.

Automobile Liability

This coverage includes other people's property, other automobiles, persons in other vehicles, and persons in the insured automobile. If you are using your personal car for business purposes, exclusively or occasionally, it is important that you have your premium cover business use. Problems can arise if you have an accident and it is discovered that your car was indeed used for business purposes. In America, "deep pockets" mentality prevails. Should you have an accident with a company vehicle, the injured always go after the business as well as the driver personally, because most businesses have a higher net worth and value than an individual. For their injured clients, attorneys look everywhere for sources of monetary awards.

Fire, Flood, and Theft Liability

If you operate your firm out of your home, you probably have fire and theft insurance. If you start your firm in an office outside your home, it is important to get coverage. Make sure that your fire coverage also covers your documents. Attempting to replace stolen or burned drawings or computer files is nearly impossible. Always keep a set of computer disks of your financial, word processing, and CADD files off-site, away from your office. Backup your data everyday. Better safe than sorry.

Overhead Expense Insurance

This insurance covers the costs of fixed business expenses or overhead during your absence as a result of an illness or accident. As a start-up, it may be difficult or expensive to obtain coverage.

Personal Disability Insurance

There is a remote chance that you could become disabled for a short or long period of time. This insurance pays a certain monthly amount if you are permanently disabled, or a portion of that amount if you are partially disabled. There are short-term and long-term policies available. Check with your broker about your coverage options and premiums.

Key Person Insurance

Your death or that of your partner or associate could seriously affect the earning power of your firm. If the key person dies, your existing clients may lose confidence, leading to the loss of future commissions, erosion of competitive position, loss of revenue, and the added expense of finding and/or training a replacement. Proceeds of the key person policy, with the firm as beneficiary, are generally not subject to income taxes. However, premiums are not a deductible business expense. These funds could help you get through a difficult time of continuing your firm's growth without your partner.

Partners or Shareholders Insurance

Insurance for partners or major shareholders in a corporation is normally part of a buy-sell agreement, which allows surviving partners or shareholders to purchase the deceased's interest in the company. In the absence of a buy-sell agreement funded by life insurance, the death of a partner could cause the immediate dissolution of the partnership in law. In the case of a corporation, without a buy-sell agreement the deceased shareholder's interest is considered an asset and goes to a beneficiary outlined in the deceased's will (if a will exists) or to the state. Most states have certain quotas requiring that designers make up the majority of stockholders in a design corporation. This could prohibit an unlicensed spouse from commanding the firm. However, why take the chance and have to deal with the consequences later? You should insure your partners for at least the value of their stock in the company. You don't want to get caught in a legal battle with your former partner's spouse and/or family in the firm's valuation, let alone have to pay for their deceased spouse/parent's value.

Business Loan Insurance

In many cases, your bank will require you to have insurance coverage for the outstanding amount of your loan and will incorporate the premium payments into the loan payment. In the event of your untimely death, the outstanding balance of your loan will be paid off.

Term Life Insurance

Term life insures a person for a specified time period and then terminates. The most common period is five years. If the insured dies within the time period, the face value of the policy is paid to the beneficiaries. Since term life insurance does not have a cash or loan value, it is significantly less expensive than whole life insurance.

Medical Insurance

It is important to have sufficient medical coverage for your needs. Some designers continue the coverage provided by their former employer (check your state laws on this coverage because they vary from state to state) or, if they have a working spouse, obtain coverage on the spouse's employer's plan. Usually, health insurance is prohibitively expensive for an individual. One option is to contact your local or state AIA chapter to see if there is a group plan for designers in the region. Other trade associations may offer medical insurance to their members. Group rates are substantially less than individual rates because of the size of the group and its buying power. However, some groups require you to have four or more employees to join. Policies offered by insurance companies vary, but medical and dental plans are available for small groups. Some medical plans offer copay coverage for prescriptions, office visits, etc. Medical insurance policies are very complex. Your premiums are based on the risk value of your occupation, the amount of deductible you are willing to pay, the length of coverage during an illness, the amount of copay, and your age. Single person coverage is not inexpensive, while family coverage can be very expensive. Family coverage for children usually ends once they stop being full-time students. State laws change from year to year about medical insurance coverage. Speak with your broker. This coverage will be as expensive or more expensive than your professional liability insurance premium in your early years. Premiums can also rise at amazing rates in given years. Having medical coverage will be an attraction to prospective employees in your firm's future. When in doubt, ask your colleagues how they insure their firm's employees.

Workers' Compensation Insurance

Workers' comp requirements vary from state to state. However, when you hire employees, you will be required by your state law to provide some coverage. Usually you can obtain coverage from an independent agent as well as from the state in which you practice. This varies from state to state. Fortunately, designers are considered to be in a low-risk profession and therefore have lower-than-average rates.

PROFESSIONAL LIABILITY INSURANCE

Many designers ask the question "Why do I need professional liability insurance?" Professional liability insurance is purchased to indemnify designers for losses and costs involved in the defense of claims made against them.

Professional liability insurance covers claims arising out of errors, omissions, and negligent acts in the performance of professional design services.

There are two types of coverage:

Claims made   A claims-made policy insures only against claims made during the period of the policy.

Occurrence | Occurrence coverage provides protection against claims that are made concerning events that transpired during the policy period. The coverage will continue, even if the claim is not made until long after the event occurred and the policy period has expired.

It isn't necessary to become an expert in liability insurance. As with all other business considerations, you do need to be aware of the basics and apply common sense when making decisions. When you meet with a potential insurance agent, ask the following questions:

What will be insured under this policy?

What will not be insured under this policy?

Who is insured under this policy?

Where am I insured under this policy? (United States and Canada if applicable.)

What time frame is insured under this policy?

What is the limit of liability of this policy?

What are the insurance company's expectations of me as an insured?

How can I reduce my premiums?

What should I do if I think a claim will be made against me?

How can I become a lower risk to the insurance company?

Many designers shy away from purchasing liability insurance because of the cost of the premiums. However, if you have expectations of designing larger work or public work, the purchase of professional liability insurance will become a necessity, as it will be a requirement of the business entity or jurisdiction.

To some clients who hire designers, having professional liability insurance separates the heavyweights from the lightweights. These clients feel that having insurance shows stability as well as ability. Other clients give the impression that having liability insurance coverage is not important. They want the cheapest fee for the least expensive way to design the project. Theoretically, firms not covered by insurance will charge less for their services because their overhead is lower than that of firms with liability coverage. Look out, however, because some of those clients know what they are paying for, and others don't. Those who don't know may end up making a claim against you—even if you do not have insurance. The potential problems are costly and could even result in your bankruptcy. Paying the price for peace of mind and having coverage is the "right" way to go. Are you willing to lose your house and/or other assets due to your negligence on a project? Providing liability insurance coverage for your clients portrays the image that you are responsible, are reliable, and stand behind your work product.

How do insurance companies figure premiums on professional liability insurance? They analyze your firm's practice by project type (residential design, stadiums, commercial design, institutional design, bridges, nuclear reactors, feasibility studies, private developers as clients versus public clients, etc.). Further, they analyze the type of services that your firm offers (soil engineering, architecture, interior design, structural engineering, etc.) and its track record. The riskier the project type, the higher the premiums charged. Finally, the amount of coverage and deductible that you are willing to pay influence the premium value. Usually, premiums are based on the firm's gross revenue values. As your business grows, you can depend on your taxes and professional liability insurance premiums rising. Market trends will affect the pricing of the insurance product offerings. When the insurance market is soft (few claims), the cost of insurance will be lower than when the market is hot (many claims). The number of claims that you have encountered and the number of claims that you have paid have an influence on your premiums pricing.

Insurance companies also evaluate what your forms of contract are with your clients. Insurance companies really care about the language contained in your contracts.

The insurance companies compare your firm's results with statistics on firms similar to yours so that they can set the appropriate premium for accepting the risks of insuring your firm. Talk to your agent. Find out what other factors, if any, the insurance company considers in evaluating a design firm.

Topics to consider in your evaluation of liability carriers are: Does the company have loss prevention programs for its insureds? Does it provide seminars and training that offer continuing education credits? Does the company review your design contract language? How does it communicate current issues and trends that face design professionals and their insurance coverage?

If you cannot afford insurance at this time, plan for it. Talk to an insurance carrier and get the facts. Plan to invest your profits into a policy after the first twelve or eighteen months if possible. You will never regret it—if only for the peace of mind.

Look at it this way: In buying professional liability insurance, you have come to terms with the fact that eventually something will go wrong in your practice that will be out of your control. Having insurance protection will provide a reserve of money set aside to help cover losses incurred by the event or judgment. Procuring professional liability insurance doesn't imply that you admit you are not perfect and will make big mistakes. It does send a signal to clients and other consulting design professionals that you care and have invested in risk management to protect your new asset, your firm, just as you protect your other assets in life.

PRACTICING DESIGN WITHOUT INSURANCE

When many designers start their own firm, they decide to "go naked" and do without professional liability insurance for a period of time. If the degree of exposure is low owing to the nature of the services provided by the practice (e.g., feasibility studies, master plans), this may be a viable alternative. If you elect not to carry liability insurance and you are sued for negligence, and you have few or no personal assets (a car, a home, a retirement account, a savings account) that a judgment can be placed against, you can file for personal bankruptcy as an outcome. Bear in mind that filing for bankruptcy will affect your personal credit rating, for the present and the future. Another alternative is to form a corporation without liability insurance or assets.

If you intend to practice design without professional liability insurance, do consult your attorney to maximize protection in your particular circumstances. What protects other colleagues may not protect you.

Buying professional design liability insurance is a business decision based on several factors:

* You need to evaluate the experience, technical competency, and quality control capabilities of yourself and your partner(s). Any weak characteristics in these areas will probably lead to a potential claim in the future.

* You need to evaluate your potential client base, and what kinds of clients they are. Will they sue you for claims made?

* You must evaluate the characteristics of your potential markets. For example, condominium associations are tough on the design

profession because they are incorporated groups of people (not individuals) and they are known to sue everyone involved in the project's implementation because of faulty material performance. These groups will go after the contractor, the architect, the engineers, etc., looking for the weak link who has the deepest pockets. Many times, in these cases, the value of the time that you must invest in protecting your assets, career, and reputation far exceeds the value of the deductible that you would be responsible for paying! Public-sector clients and private companies usually require liability insurance. They will ask you to forward a certificate of coverage to them to confirm the amounts of your coverage. Residential clients usually do not require liability insurance.

If your firm will be designing small projects, you may decide that not having insurance coverage is the right way to go. However, consider that you are not perfect, and that it is not a perfect world. You cannot, as a businessperson, ignore this fact. Eventually, according to Murphy's law, something will go wrong! Here are some options to consider if you elect not to purchase liability insurance:

* Set aside profits and fund an emergency reserve each month, each year. Make it an overhead expense of the firm. Put the money into a certificate of deposit so that it will be difficult to get at when you are tempted to meet other expenses. Be committed to the vision of this protection!

* Place all assets in your spouse's name or jointly in both your names (check your state laws) to make yourself more judgment-proof in the courts.

Finally, here are two options to consider when you do plan on purchasing insurance:

* Purchase coverage commensurate with your project culture. Don't over-insure yourself.

* Purchase a policy with a reasonable and realistic deductible value that you can afford, or borrow from a lender. (Once you build your emergency reserve up to $25,000 or more, you will be better able to self-fund the deductible.)

MANAGE YOUR RISK, FOLLOW YOUR GUT

Starting a new design firm is an exciting event in your life. Dealing with risk and eventually liability issues is part of business. If you are risk averse, you need to rethink your position of starting and operating a design firm. Like it or not, you must make a decision about whether you will purchase liability insurance. Unfortunately for start-up firms, the insurance companies have the hammer. They don't know you. They don't know if you are a great designer or a bum! For an insurance company to take a risk on a new firm, the premiums must be worth its while. On average, insurance companies will charge up to 9 percent of gross revenues for new firms. For start-up sole proprietors, a premium of $6,000 to $10,000 per year is a lot of money! The longer you remain in business, and the larger you grow, the premiums as a percentage of gross revenue decrease. Firms that have five to nineteen employees pay approximately 4 to 5 percent of gross fees for premiums. Please note that these percentages are cyclical and change often due to market conditions.

The bottom line is: Manage your risk and follow your gut feeling. If you have compelling reasons not to have liability coverage for a few years, do it—but be aware and careful. Always plan to purchase insurance in the future as your firm grows. The longer you are in business, the more likely it is that you will encounter a claim. Liability insurance is certainly a double-edged sword. For many firms, it is the fourth most expensive overhead item—behind payroll, health insurance, and rent. While most firms do not like paying for it, they also hope that they will never have to use it!

1 0
OFFICE AND EQUIPMENT CONSIDERATIONS

When I had to make the decision on location, I remember having two important criteria. First, I refused to work at home, because home was an apartment—and I doubted I would be disciplined enough to work so close to the refrigerator and television. Second, I had to find an office that rented for less than my apartment. Why? I don't know, it just made me more comfortable, dealing with the risk of the lease.

I'll never forget paying that first rent check to my landlord. At first, I was very proud of this important event; however, as soon as I wrote the amount, I immediately thought of the next twenty-three checks I would be writing in the future. That is a lot of money! Can I afford to rent this office? Is it the correct image for my firm? Is the landlord going to clean the space properly? I have to write another one of these checks in thirty days. I sure hope some of my clients pay me beforehand!

WHERE IS THE RIGHT LOCATION FOR YOUR FIRM?

How do you determine the "right" location for your new office? The first hurdle to jump is the home office versus outside-the-home office dilemma. There is nothing more financially attractive than having an office in your home. The cost of the rent is right (included in your mortgage if you have one, or your rent if you are renting space) and the IRS allows you to write off part of the expense on your tax return. It can be a real winner for some designers. A home office is convenient—you can roll right out of bed into the studio in a matter of minutes! No rush-hour traffic to deal with, no problems finding a parking space, no bad weather to fight! The home office saves travel time. (How many people do you know who travel more than an hour a day to the office? That's five or more potential billable hours per week if you work out of your home!)

Working at home is becoming a way of life for many business technology advances. As long as you have a phone and e-mail, the world is your oyster. Armed with a phone, e-mail, and a computer, you can do business anywhere in the world. Many designers who work out of their home say that they schedule all or a majority of their meetings at the client's office—not because they do not wish the client to see their office and its location but because clients appreciate the "level of service" of a designer who comes to them! Working out of your home also has its disadvantages. One is image. Do you want to have your clients meet with you in your kitchen, or your office in the basement or on the second floor? For some practitioners, this is acceptable. For others, it poses an image problem. Another disadvantage of the home office is the presence of so many distractions—the refrigerator, the television, and so on. If you practice where you live, do you ever really leave the office? Many designers want a space away from home so that, at the end of the day, they can close the door and go through the ritual of driving home, away from the studio. Finally, you need to check your local jurisdiction's zoning laws to see if a home office is permitted in your area.

Another issue with a home office is the question of whether you want future employees coming to and working in your home space. This can be difficult. Having an office in the basement, in the garage, or in a guesthouse are all logical, viable options. However, sharing a den or a dining room with staff could be challenging. It can be difficult when you are encountering deadlines, and staff are within your home after midnight or even pulling an all-nighter. If you are to go to bed while they are working there, are they trustworthy to be left alone in your home? And what is the perception of you going to bed and requiring them to remain awake working?

To work out of your home requires discipline to help separate business from home life. You have to make the right decision for yourself and your new company—its vision and image. Some designers work out of their home for a period of time to develop a firm foundation for their new company, and then move into office space outside the home. Other designers want to separate their office from their home at the outset, even though costs get in the way. They forge ahead anyway, some with reckless abandon. Should you choose to work out of your home in the beginning, the best decision you can make is to establish a time-parameter goal. Try to move out of your home in twelve or eighteen months, or sooner if possible. This will provide a target for success. Consider your initial studio space to be your "incubator." At some point you need to move on. Planning for growth and a move is very healthy, portraying vision and success.

Many a designer overspends to outfit an office to present a particular image. Rome wasn't built in a day. Think before you act, and be reasonable in your approach to outfitting your new space. Chances are that you will schedule more of your client meetings outside your office than in it. Keep your fix-up costs simple in the beginning to portray a cost-conscious designer image, and invest your valuable capital on items that will make you profitable—staff, a computer, or other equipment. Design your office space to be commensurate and consistent with your new image.

Designers don't receive commissions because they have unique, wonderful offices. In a few years, when you are successful and grow, you will move on. Your tastes will change, and all that you invested in that trendy office will be out the window. Invest your money in your spatial needs wisely. Don't let your design ego get in the way! Design your space to be comfortable and effective in a business manner. You will be spending a fair amount of time in this new office, so you might as well invest wisely and create a space that will inspire you and your upcoming staff to be the best that you can be.

Many designers have opportunities to locate their new, small quarters in a consultant's office, a contractor's office, or a developer's office building. Before you commit to any "opportunities," which may include free rent or bartered rent, consider the image of the location and whether it will give the impression that you are being "kept" and are not truly independent. Ask a colleague to evaluate the opportunity. Ask for advice. But only you can make the decision.

Some designers look for an office with complimentary professional or business support capabilities. Essentially, you have your own office with your own furniture, but the rent expenses of the overall office and the receptionist's salary are shared on a proportional basis with all the tenants. Secretarial expenses are negotiated according to use. Usually, telephone answering services and computer networking are available. If you do seek out a pooling arrangement, try to have a minimal notice period to end your lease. You may wish to leave because of expansion, inability to pay the rent, or personality conflicts. Make sure that the terms of your rental relationship are simple and in writing. Try to negotiate a month-to-month lease for maximum flexibility.

You can see how important a decision on office location is. For many, the decision is driven by economics at first. The funny thing about economics is that for as long as you are in business, you will wonder: "Can I afford to be located where I am? Is it the correct image? Does the space meet the company's vision?" This isn't something that happens only when you start up. You are not alone. It is an ongoing process!

HOW DO YOU NEGOTIATE A LEASE FOR A SPACE?

The search for office space can be very demanding but also very exciting. Many points need to be considered in researching space. The first decision to make is whether or not to retain the services of a real estate broker. You may find space by observing signage identifying the spatial opportunity. You may discover space through word of mouth while networking. Or, you can retain the services of a commercial broker, who works in the space market in your area every day, and can give you a written summary of spatial considerations. Some brokers, being full service, can assist you in identifying space, touring it, negotiating lease terms, and being there as your paid consultant. No matter which way you go, ultimately, you must be comfortable with your decisions on location, parking, rent, utility costs, etc. If you are uncomfortable with the variables in the leasing equation, lean on your leasing agent to work things out and assist you in successfully obtaining the right space for you.

Leasing space has its challenges, and it is important that you consult with your accountant and lawyer as well as your real estate broker (should you elect to have one) before signing anything. Don't be surprised if your lease agreement goes back and forth between landlord and lessee (you) several times. You should shop around for space before you negotiate—to make sure that you understand the market price and offerings and that you have the best arrangement for your needs. Smaller commercial leases generally have terms from one to five years. There are three types of lease payment formulas:

Net leases
Double net leases
Triple net leases

A net lease means that the base rent is the total rent. Double net is similar, except you must pay a pro rata share of any of the landlord's property tax increase over the term of your lease on an annual basis. A triple net lease includes the rent, taxes, insurance, maintenance, repairs, improvements, management, and administration fees passed on by the landlord to the tenants.

Here are some tips on negotiating a lease:

1. Rather than negotiate a three-year lease, ask for a one-year lease with two additional one-year options. You minimize your risk if you can't pay or if you outgrow the space.

2. Consider offering the last two or three months' rent as a deposit. If you default the lease and leave before the end of the term, the deposit monies go to the landlord, and you are free of any further liability.

3. In a renter's market, try to get the landlord to pay for all your tenant improvements.

4. Ask for "free rent" terms in your lease to help offset start-up overhead costs.

5. Try to get out of paying the last month's security deposit rent, if possible. If not, get the landlord to pay you interest at a fixed rate for the term of the lease.

The location and setup of your business office is more important than you may think. It affects how you will perform your tasks every day. Its quality will speak volumes about who you are as a person, and as a design firm. Perception is reality. A great rule of thumb is to not spend more than 5 percent of your overall annual budget on occupancy (your lease and expenses). If your business plan estimates your annual volume to be $500,000 the first year, then you can afford an annual rent of $25,000 or $2,083.00 per month. If you exceed this rule of thumb, realize that the firm's profits—return to you as the owner—may suffer. Occupancy is a major issue to deal with, yet it should be only 5 percent of your annual expenses. Obtaining "balance" is key in finding and developing new space for the new firm. Location, rental rate, size, and quality of the space all factor into your decision. You must learn to balance all of these factors to obtain the right space for you and your new firm.

As designers, few of us are trained in real estate lease transactions. Be comfortable with yourself and your decisions. Develop and maintain balance in how your new firm and space will relate to each other. If something doesn't seem right, it isn't.

EQUIPPING YOUR NEW OFFICE

Now that you have made your commitment regarding office space, what will you need in the way of equipment to operate your new firm? The answer lies in how much equipment you presently own and how much money you have to spend.

Think about the firm that you just left. Does it have any old equipment that it would be willing to sell or give to you? To start out, make a list of the basics: computer hardware and software, telephone/cellular phone, reference table (board), reference material, lamps, conference table, office supplies, telephone answering machine, and so on. Chart 13 presents an extensive list.

Each one of us is different. We have different backgrounds, computer skills, priorities, and goals. The fact of the matter is that you can spend very little or thousands of dollars on start-up equipment. The decisions are hard, but be true to yourself. Delay the purchase of some equipment if you can, and spend the money saved on more important, less expensive equipment. For example, should you purchase or lease a photocopying machine when you start your firm? Would the money be better spent on another purchase if you could lease space in a building or an office with a photocopier next door that you could operate for 10 cents a copy? Must you purchase or lease a fax machine on the first day of your new business? Again, can you utilize the business fax next door for a while? Be wise in planning your equipment purchases. In today's business world, having a cellular/digital phone, a laptop/PC with the right software, and Web access is most of what you need to communicate when you open up your studio. Purchase or lease equipment when you really need it. Otherwise, why spend the money?

COMPUTERIZATION

Many years ago, when I wrote the first edition of this book, I asked the question, "Do you need a computer on the first day of your business?" The answer to this question depends on your generational position, your open-mindedness to technological advances, and your literacy on the computer. However, in today's IT world, you cannot open a design business without one.

Computers are incredible assistants for small business as well as business in general. However, should you spend hundreds or thousands of dollars on accounting software if you are going to do only twenty projects and invoice $100,000 in the first year? Computers are constantly changing for the better.

CHART 13
Typical Business Equipment

Equipment	Cost/Buy/ lease	Time frame/ Present	Near future	Future
Accounting software				
Batteries				
Bookshelves for library				
Business cards				
CADD hardware				
CADD software				
CADD 3D animation software				
CADD station table				
Digital camera				
Chairs				
Coffeemaker				
Computer paper				
Computer printers				
Conference table				
Copy paper (8.5" × 11" and 11" × 17")				
Database software				
Desktop publishing software				
Dictation/recording equipment				
Sketching/drafting equipment				
Envelopes				
Facsimile machine				
File cabinets				
Flashlight				
Flat files				
DVD/CD storage units				
Folders				
Glue, rubber cement				
Laptop computer				
Lamps				
Laser printer				

(Continued)

Equipment	Cost/Buy/ lease	Time frame/ Present	Near future	Future
Letterhead				
Mailing labels				
Cellular/digital/mobile phone				
Modem				
Mouse				
PC				
Personal data assistant				
Paperclip holders				
Paper cutter				
Pencils				
Pencil holders				
Pencil sharpener				
Pens				
Post-it note pads				
Postage machine				
Photocopier				
Scale for postage				
Scissors				
SF254/255 software				
Spray adhesive, spray mount				
Spreadsheet software				
Stapler				
Large stapler for drawings				
Scoth/double-coated/ drafting tape				
Tape dispenser				
Tape measures (25' and 100')				
Tape recorder				
Telephone system				
Telephone voice mail system				
Three-hole punch				
Time management system				
Two-hole punch for files				
White-out				
Word-processing software				

As soon as you purchase one, it is outdated! Remember, once you make a commitment to hardware and software, you must always upgrade to stay current with speed and accuracy.

Purchase a computer system that you are comfortable with. You have been utilizing software for years, so you know what is right for you. As for hardware, going with a PC or laptop depends on how much processing power you need. Is mobility important for you? For millions of users in the world, Apple users swear by Apple, and Windows users swear by their operating system. It is up to you and the type of computer individual you are. Both systems can operate software recommended for design firms.

Software applications for the start-up design firm should include word processing and spreadsheets at the minimum. You may consider incorporating an accounting software package as well. Be a smart shopper when it comes to computer hardware and software. Talk to your colleagues and find out what they recommend. Learn from their war stories, and try to avoid their mistakes. Many computer stores offer hardware with software already loaded on the hard drives. A variety of word-processing, spreadsheet, and accounting software exists, so be comfortable with your decision. Beware of software that is too complex for your new operation. For example, you do not need accounting software designed for a fifty-person firm! It may be years before you get to that number. There is no status in overpaying! Purchase a system that will work for a firm of up to twenty staff.

Other software available for design firms includes master specification formats, databases, desktop publishing, CADD, and 3D Animation programs. If you have never been trained in CADD software, you had better learn it or have someone in your start-up who has. If you have a background in CADD and are "one to one" (have extensive knowledge and experience and can work effectively on it), and if you can afford a CADD station with software and plotter, then go for it! The fact of the matter is that if you are not "one to one" on CADD when you start your firm, you won't have the time to be trained on it. Also, many designers purchase a CADD system but do not buy a plotter to save money at the initial purchase. Their goal is to add the plotter later, and utilize a consultant's plotter or a reproduction house's plotter at present. Remember, there is a fair amount of risk involved in using another firm's hardware and plotters. The formats must be compatible, and you must coordinate your deadlines with their availability. If you can't afford a comprehensive CADD system, think twice before you act.

Another key decision is whether you should purchase a desktop or laptop computer to work from. Most businesses have conventional PCs in their offices. Laptops are the future of PCs, and are here now. New models appear almost daily, with faster and faster hard drives and memory. The benefit of a laptop is the transportability of the unit. You can work on it at home, in the office, on a train, in an airplane, or even in a client's office. Laptops offer the most flexibility. Some designers even have CADD on their laptops to make adjustments to files in the field, on a job site, or in the client's office. In the past, you might have had one computer that lived in the office, and you might also have had a home computer. Now the laptop platform allows you to purchase one system and use it everywhere. PCs also have wireless modems to link with other PCs and databases. Many designers use wireless modems in their laptops when they travel to stay in touch with the office and data. Once again, before you make a purchase of a laptop or standard PC, talk with your friends and colleagues. Conduct your research, and help reduce your risk in making the right computer decision for yourself.

Computers are the backbone of the design professions today. Computerization of a business requires a total commitment to remain up-to-date and be successful. A common complaint of small design firm owners is the expense of computerization. PCs for word-processing, spreadsheet, and accounting applications are affordable, but CADD-based PC systems are expensive. A good rule of thumb is to commit to budget approximately 7 percent of your annual revenue toward computerization that your firm needs.

Make your decision regarding technology before you jump out of the airplane. Again, it will become increasingly difficult to get trained in software after you have started the firm, since its operation will dominate your every waking moment. If you get through the learning curve before you open your new business, you will find that the business and professional software will smooth your firm's growth transitions, speed your operations to make the firm more profitable, and in the big picture lead your firm more rapidly to success!

TELEPHONE EQUIPMENT

The telephone is perhaps the single most important piece of equipment in an office. All of us take this simple late-nineteenth-century invention for granted. Today, cellular and digital telecommunications have revolutionized our being reachable. Since we live in the information age, the telephone will become more and more advanced and sophisticated in the business world. Just think of it. It wasn't long ago that "touch tone" phones were introduced, and today we not only call others from our cars, trains, and airplanes but instant message, text message, and forward photographs from our phones.

As your firm grows, you may want to consider a fixed, permanent phone system for your office or studio. In selecting a telephone system, remember who you are—your firm's size—and be realistic in your search for the most important piece of equipment in your new office. Your phone system, whether it is a single phone or a system that can be expanded to one hundred phones, is your direct connection to the outside business world. Make sure that the phone you buy is reliable and serviceable. If you start your firm in your home, your local telephone service provider may offer an optional residential service plan for "unlimited" service. However, if you rent office space and start your firm in a commercial center, the telecommunications provider will charge you for each and every phone call that you place from your office. You will notice this on your monthly bill. In the phone company's view, American business "pays the freight" for the cost of operating the telecommunications network in our country, and the residential consumer gets the "free ride." At first, you will feel compelled to keep track of how many calls you make daily, to check the phone company's computer accuracy. The sad news is that the computer is virtually infallible! Remember to get a great, reliable phone at first, and worry about expansion and those other "extra" features later. Investing in a "call waiting" system instead of buying another telephone line will save you money. Adding "call forwarding" will allow you to operate out of two separate areas and will give the impression of being totally accessible.

Finally, when you are just starting out and probably can't afford a receptionist, voice mail is a must. Many of us claim that we hate leaving voice mail but, let's face it, voice mail has become mainstream in our world of communications. An alternative to voice mail is a telephone answering service. These services are available just about everywhere, and offer a "real person" to answer your phone. After a while, however, your clients will notice that a different person answers your phone on different days, and that whenever "they" answer, you are not in. Many clients complain that these services are as impersonal as the notorious answering machine. Also, an answering service is a monthly expense. Finally, voice mail boxes may be offered by your telecommunications provider with competitive rates. You make the recording, and you can access the messages anytime and anywhere. Contact your provider for details.

MOBILE PHONES/MOBILE E-MAIL

Many people who feel that accessibility is the key to success find that mobile phones and e-mail are the life saver of business. It is true that clients appreciate (and even demand) being able to reach you at a moment's notice. However, it is possible to be too accessible! If you give your cell phone number to clients, they expect a return phone call within minutes of paging you. Talk about expectations!

There are numerous cellular and digital telecommunications providers. Make sure that you consider several options, and discuss the pros and cons of each with your friends and colleagues before you make your commitment.

Mobile e-mail has become a necessity for many over the past few years. This can be an expensive form of staying in touch with your clients, family, staff, and friends. However, if you travel during the day and being responsive to your client's needs is your passion, you really cannot do without this valuable communication tool. Being able to view Word documents and spreadsheet data away from the office or studio, on the job site, or away on vacation is amazing.

Manage your accessibility. Manage your client's expectations!

If people despise voice mail, they feel just as strongly about cell phones going off in the middle of a meeting. It is true that phones now come with varying options of alert, from a single beep to a vibration, to an annoyingly loud beep to music options. Many businesspeople who wear cell phone/ mobile e-mail devices do so for various reasons. Some refuse to delegate, and must be involved in every decision in their firm. Therefore, they want to be contacted regarding any issue. If you are out of the office for great periods of time and you have an assistant, the cell phone/e-mail device can be a great communications link. Some companies use codes that can be displayed on the screen to communicate the degree of importance of a beep. Selecting a personal data assistant, cell phone, or mobile e-mail device is a personal, expensive decision. See more about this item, below.

Your office telephone communications will grow naturally with the growth and success of your firm. Remember to keep a level head and to base your decisions about equipment purchases on real need, not perceived need or ego!

PERSONAL DATA ASSISTANTS

These devices have exploded in popularity over the past ten years. Not only will they organize your calendar, to-do list, and memos of information, but they can process your e-mail and serve as your telephone communications tool. Most importantly, they sync with your computer. PDAs are an invaluable tool in today's business climate. Palm and Blackberry are two such devices that are popular. Check with your cellular or digital phone provider, as well as friends and colleagues, to see which product is the correct one for your needs.

FINALLY

Stay on top of technological improvements/enhancements created for design firms. Don't be on the "bleeding edge" but near the "cutting edge." Listen to your colleagues. Attend your design association meetings on technology to keep up with the pack. Keeping your new firm's backbone healthy will help supply the profits that you will need to grow.

We have examined many issues that you must consider and address in starting up your firm. Some designers find the number of issues overwhelming and decide not to start. Others overcome their intimidation by sharing their concerns with one or more partners.

As human beings, we start life learning to breath involuntarily. As we mature, we gain confidence in crawling, standing up, walking, running, driving, skiing. The more we do, the more confidence we gain. If we began worrying about every little thing that might go wrong, we wouldn't get out of bed in the morning! Starting a business is a similar journey. We may not do things right the first time, but as long as we learn from our mistakes, we will endure and succeed.

If you think you are the first person to face these issues, rest assured that you are not, and will not be, alone! Every person who founds an organization deals with the same uncertainties. If you try to handle multiple issues simultaneously, you will become confused and disenchanted. You must proceed in an organized, timely, logical, and practical fashion. Begin now to organize your thoughts as you plan your new venture's home.

PART 3 : Getting Down to Business

"EFFECTIVE LEADERSHIP IS PUTTING FIRST THINGS FIRST. EFFECTIVE MANAGEMENT IS DISCIPLINE, CARRYING IT OUT."
—*Stephen Covey*

"REGARD IT AS JUST AS DESIRABLE TO BUILD A CHICKEN HOUSE AS TO BUILD A CATHEDRAL."
—*Frank Lloyd Wright*

"TRY, TRY, TRY, AND KEEP ON TRYING IS THE RULE THAT MUST BE FOLLOWED TO BECOME AN EXPERT IN ANYTHING."
—*W. Clement Stone*

"THE FIRST RESPONSIBILITY OF A LEADER IS TO DEFINE REALITY. THE LAST IS TO SAY THANK YOU. IN BETWEEN, THE LEADER IS A SERVANT."
—*Max de Pree*

11
DEVELOPING PRELIMINARY BUSINESS AND MARKETING PLANS

"The secret of business is to know something that nobody else knows."

—ARISTOTLE ONASSIS

"A good plan violently executed now is better than a perfect plan executed next week."

—GEORGE S. PATTON

"Our goals can only be reached through a vehicle of a plan, in which we must fervently believe, and upon which we must vigorously act. There is no other route to success."

—PABLO PICASSO

"I try to learn from the past, but I plan for the future by focusing exclusively on the present. That's were the fun is."

—DONALD TRUMP

WHAT IS A BUSINESS PLAN?
A business plan is a written summary of what you hope to accomplish by being in business and how you intend to organize your resources to meet your goals. It is an essential guide for operating your business successfully and measuring your progress along the way.

Why Prepare a Business Plan?

Starting and owning your own design firm isn't easy. There are no magic formulas or special buttons to push that can guarantee success. However, there are some fundamentals that give the entrepreneur designer a better chance of succeeding. One of the fundamentals is good planning. Most designers prefer to be designers first and businesspeople second. However, planning and management skills are vital to business success. As in anything else in life, those who do not plan well run a very high risk of failure. If you do not know where you are going in your personal or your business life, there is little chance that you will arrive anywhere content and successful.

Developing a business is much like building a building. As designers, we know that a building will be successful only if its planning stages culminate in the "right" design that works for the client. Hundreds of decisions go into the building design. We are trained in design school and during our internships to build our ideas on a sound base and then, step by step, to develop a justified approach to a design solution. The "right" design doesn't occur on the first attempt, though most designers know that the first concept is often 90 percent "there."

Much like designing a building, establishing and operating a business requires hundreds of decisions. From day to day, a businessperson must develop a sound base, and step by step develop logical approaches to the challenges that everyday business life poses.

The most important aspect of a building is the construction of its foundation. The entire success of the project (will the building stand up?) depends on the foundation. Yet, after excavation, construction, and backfill, no one physically sees the foundation of the building. It is expected and taken for granted that the foundation will work. The "success" of the building is judged instead on its aesthetic value and function.

In business, people see you, your logo, and the product of your design, but they rarely see your business plan (your foundation). Other businesspeople— bankers, accountants, lawyers, and clients—fully expect that you have a business plan. Like a foundation it is never seen, but it is taken for granted, because your firm should do a good job and succeed. Planning the future forces you to think ahead with vision; it encourages realistic thinking instead of overoptimism. It helps you identify potential markets, income strategies, and other competitive conditions under which you will operate. The great thing about developing a business plan is discovering new opportunities as well as weaknesses in your firm and your vision.

Having clear goals and a well-written business plan will help you make critical decisions and stay focused on your charted course. Your goals can always be altered—provided you have a documented business plan that enables you to evaluate the alternatives you will encounter day to day.

Write your plan with two purposes in mind:

1. The plan is a working document of how you are going to build your design firm.

2. The plan is also a sales document to bankers and clients, helping to communicate your vision and organizational skills.

A successful business plan achieves the following:

- It organizes objectives.

- It develops strategies for accomplishing those objectives.

- It sets priorities.

- It helps set schedules and timetables.

- It sacrifices activities and delegates responsibilities.

- It anticipates problems.

- It creates solutions.

- It sets financial guidelines and goals.

Two out of three preliminary business plans ignore the first goal of organizing objectives. They therefore become weak selling tools for the businesses. Ten percent of ongoing business plans lose sight of the organizational goal and instead become complex, boring, unreadable documents that serve no purpose other than to be recycled.

Every large city has companies that specialize in writing business plans for firms. For a fee ranging from $1,500 to $25,000, their experts will interview you, develop drafts for your review, and incorporate your comments into the final product. However, if you were to request five copies of "individual" plans developed by a particular firm, you would notice a sameness about them. The wording and clauses have the same ring, the ratios are always ideal, the graphics appear similar, the milestones overlap, and even the formats and covers look the same.

Your banker reads many business plans every year and can easily spot a "proposal company's" product. Such a formula plan is a signal that the firm hasn't taken the time to develop its own plan (no matter how much was spent for the proposal). The bank is likely to regard it as a pretext for borrowing money. Bankers rarely give a "processed" business plan much attention because it is generic, impersonal, and homogenized.

It is critical, therefore, that you write your plan yourself. If you utilize another design firm's plan, you will become lazy in thinking about your own, and you may unthinkingly plagiarize wording, formats, and graphics. Force yourself to sit down and think about your goals and how you really are. You will be amazed at how easy the exercise becomes if you stick to a simple thinking and writing process.

When starting your firm, keep your business plan direct and to the point. You have a lifetime in business to refine, redefine, expand, and change your objectives. The preliminary plan should summarize your goals and objectives, and serve as an outline for a formal business plan. The preliminary plan is an abridged version, maybe 10 percent of the final's size. It is important, however, to address all the variables outlined in the recommended format below.

Format of the Business Plan

A business plan normally consists of five parts:

Introduction
The firm's concept
The firm's operation
The financial plan
Appendix

A business plan always starts with an introduction, a brief executive summary that captures the excitement of your new firm and attracts the immediate attention of the potential lender or client.

The firm's concept describes what your new design firm does, identifies your firm's market potential, and outlines your goals and action plan for the coming year. Make sure that your stated business goals are realistic and in line with your financial goals, management ability, and personal and family considerations. The heart of the firm's concept is your monthly business forecast for the coming year. The business forecast forms the basis for your cash flow and projected income statement. It also assesses risks that you may encounter and outlines contingency plans.

The firm's operation summarizes your location (advantages and disadvantages), size (advantages and disadvantages), leasehold improvements, image and personality to be projected (and how you intend to do so), and hours of operation. The financial plan outlines your present financial status and potential needs. This section should be brief, outlining your expected fees, costs, and profits for the year. The outline will serve as a benchmark for comparisons in the future.

Finally, the appendix should include items such as these:

Personal financial statement
Letters of intent from new clients
Summary of business insurance policies
Accounts receivable summary (if available)
Accounts payable summary (if available)
Summary of legal agreements
Copy of company brochure
List of references
Copies of news articles about the firm

Chart 14 presents a detailed checklist of points to be covered in your plan. Remember, formulating the plan is a cumulative process. Don't expect to isolate yourself, sit down, and in six hours bang out a complete plan. Remember, grow into it!

After reading all this, you may be saying to yourself, "My firm doesn't need a loan from a bank—I have my life savings to fall back on. I have an angel spouse and family with 'deep pockets' as a funding source, a safety net. I don't need a business plan, preliminary or final! Why take the time to write something that I know I will be doing my best at on a day-to-day basis? I can't predict the future anyway. I'm a designer, not a writer or businessperson!"

The fact of the matter is that simply thinking and writing down your ideas is half the battle! Even the shortest, most personalized business plan will gain respect from your banker. You may not need the bank's money now, but what about in the future? Your private lending sources (safety nets) may change. Growth is a challenging process that devours cash. Assets such as computers shouldn't be paid for in cash or out of cash flow. They should be financed because of the tax advantages that such funding offers. Remember, business is a game. Most companies follow the same rules to achieve success. Eventually, your banker will become as important a player in the game as your account-ant, lawyer, and insurance agent.

Imagine a contractor trying to construct a building without a set of plans and specifications! Now imagine trying to build a design firm without a business plan. Don't do it!

CHART 14
Business Plan Checklist

I. INTRODUCTION
Company name
Address
Telephone number
Facsimile
Web address
E-mail address
Contact person
Paragraph about company
    Nature of design and market area
Financial needs
    Term loan, operating line of credit, mortgage, etc.
Summary of proposed use of funds

II. THE FIRM'S CONCEPT

Summary on one page
> Highlights/executive summary

Table of contents
Design profession outlook and growth potential
General markets
The competition
National and economic trends
Business goals
> One-year
> Two/three-year outlook
> Long-term: five-year

Marketing plan
> Experience
> Target markets

Forecasts
> One month
> First year
> Midrange
> Long range

III. THE FIRM'S OPERATION

Location and space
Staffing required
Equipment required
Business structure
> Sole proprietorship
> Partnership
> Corporation

List of officers
List of contracts with clients
Background of key person(s)
Organization chart

Action plan
  Steps to accomplish this year's goals
  Schedule outlining checkpoints throughout year

IV. THE FINANCIAL PLAN
Financial forecast
Preliminary balance sheet
Income and expense forecast statement
Cash flow forecast
Financing needs (if necessary)
  Loans

V. APPENDIX
List of references
  Banker
  Leasing agent
  Accountant
  Attorney
  Insurance agent
Personal net worth statement
Summary of business insurance coverage
Accounts receivable summary
Accounts payable summary
Legal agreements
Financial statements for company
Copy of company brochure
News articles on firm

SAMPLE BUSINESS PLAN

Chart 15 presents a sample business plan for a design firm based on the outline presented in this chapter. Use the plan as a guide in developing your new firm's business plan.

CHART 15
Sample Business Plan

APPLE ARCHITECTURE, INC.
ARCHITECTURE/INTERIOR DESIGN–BUSINESS PLAN: 2006

I. BACKGROUND
Company name: Apple Architecture, Inc.
Address: 401 Orchard Avenue
                Applegrove, Maryland 20000
Telephone: (000) 000–0000
Facsimile: (000) 000–0000
Web site: www.Applearch.com
Contact person: George MacIntosh Apple IV, AIA President
E-mail: gma@applearch.com

The Company
Apple Architecture, Inc. has provided quality architecture and interior design services throughout the Middle Atlantic region since 2000. The company was founded with a portfolio of mostly residential and small commercial projects. Through the early 2000s, the firm strove to develop and maintain a commercial and institutional client base, which expanded throughout the East Coast markets. With the expected downturn in the economy, the firm began concentrating in 2005 on developing a strong institutional client base, including government, healthcare, and educational commissions. The company still maintains a strong residential design portfolio in the multifamily, single-family speculative, custom, and addition markets.

II. BUSINESS CONCEPT
Outlook
The outlook of the architectural profession in the Middle Atlantic region is one of "steady no-growth." The current recession has hit the area, with many firms downsizing. It has been said in the design industry that "the

recovery is here," and that the business volume and size of a firm at present will be the size of the firm for the near future.

The small-scale residential design market is strong, along with institutional clients (healthcare, education, and government). Apple Architecture, Inc., does not expect significant growth over the next year; however, after staff reductions in the past two years, we do expect to conduct limited staff increases in our CADD group.

The Competition

Apple Architecture, Inc., with a staff of twelve, is considered in the profession as a "medium-sized" architectural firm. As of January 2006, 9 percent of the architectural firms nationwide are our size. Some 86 percent of the firms have fewer than ten employees, and 5 percent have more than twenty staff positions. On a national basis, medium-sized firms control 17 percent of the market share of the gross billings.

The recession has created quite an erosion in the profession. Many of the larger firms have reduced staff, which has created many smaller, "one-person" firms.

Our firm has found that it is now competing with the start-up firms on smaller-scale projects. The "larger firms" are now competing for our "larger" projects, which is a challenge in and of itself.

We feel that we are in an excellent position because, given our size and experience, we can still compete on all levels and get "our share" of commissions. We have significantly reduced our overhead to compete with the competition and remain profitable.

Business Goals

Foremost, Apple Architecture, Inc., wants to be a profitable, service-driven design firm. We have managed our practice through the good as well as the difficult times over the past decade. What we have learned in the past twenty months has been how to control our cost of business and maintain a profit through the lean times.

Because of the economy and available developed structures, the construction industry will be heavily concentrated in the renovation and interiors markets over the next five to ten years. We started our interiors division five years ago, expecting it to grow, to hedge our business in the lean "design" times ahead. The interiors work is profitable, and is helping open doors into the healthcare industry. We expect our interiors group to make and possibly exceed the 30 percent volume of the firm by year-end.

Our long-term business plan is to have an established design firm, noted for its quality service and commitment to the community and environment, and to be a leader of the profession in the Maryland marketplace. We see a similarity in the profession's future to that of the 1960s and 1970s, when there were not as many firms and most of the work was institutionally oriented.

Apple Architecture, Inc., has been in a survival mode over the past year; however, we do see a brighter future, unlike the 1980s, with more stable and rewarding times through community-oriented projects. The role of designers as problem solvers to the government and society will increase during the challenging decade of the 2000s. We at Apple Architecture, Inc., are proud to be in our "position."

Forecasts

Apple Architecture, Inc. enjoyed its highest-gross volume year in 2005. We concentrated on reducing our overhead throughout the year, and invested our profits into reducing our payables to consulting engineers and vendors.

The first half of 2006 has been challenging; however, owing to our decreased operational costs, we have been profitable.

Our current workload and contracts include the following:

Apple Elementary School addition for Apple County

Apple County Public Safety Headquarters

These should result in a $1 to $1.2 million gross volume year, down from $1.4 million in 2005.

III. BUSINESS OPERATION

Location

Apple Architecture, Inc. operates its business from a 6,000-gross-square-foot office building located at 401 Orchard Avenue, Applegrove, Maryland.

This central Apple County location provides our firm with unparalleled access to our client base in Apple City, Apple County, MacIntosh County, and Winesap County. We have easy access to the interstate highway system for providing service throughout the state. The firm is in year two of a five-year lease on the premises. We feel that this current office space will fulfill the needs of our staff and clientele through 2009.

Staff

Apple Architecture, Inc., currently has a staff of twelve. Of that number, five are licensed architects and one is a certified interior designer. George Apple, AIA is licensed in Maryland, Pennsylvania, Delaware, Virginia, and the District of Columbia. He is NCARB certified. Our staff has over one hundred years combined experience. Please refer to our corporate background for further detailed information.

Business Structure

Apple Architecture, Inc., has been a Maryland corporation since 2000. Officers:

George M. Apple IV, AIA President

Kyle Granny Smith, AIA Vice President

Kolby B. Apple, Secretary

Korey MacIntosh, Treasurer

WHAT IS A MARKETING PLAN?

A marketing plan is a written summary of how you intend to market your firm. It is an essential guide for planning the future of the firm and measuring its progress. Writing a marketing plan is not difficult. As a matter of fact, the most difficult task is simply sitting down and doing it!

Why Prepare a Marketing Plan?

If you polled one hundred design firms in the United States today, fewer than forty would have a documented marketing plan. And probably half of those firms haven't updated their plans in over a year.

So why prepare a plan? As with the preliminary business plan, it is important to focus on your thoughts and visions, and to document them.

Don't be scared, and don't think that once you document your ideas they cannot change. Having clear marketing objectives will help you make critical decisions and stay focused on your charted course of business. As with the business plan, there are two goals to keep in mind:

1. Keep the marketing plan simple. It is a working document that must be flexible to allow for change.

2. The plan is also a sales document to bankers and clients, communicating your vision and organizational skills.

CHART 16
Sample Marketing Plan

APPLE ARCHITECTURE, INC.
ARCHITECTURE/INTERIOR DESIGN–MARKETING PLAN: 2006

Mission Statement
Apple Architecture, Inc. will continually strive to expand its capabilities to perform larger-scale projects in the commercial, educational, and institutional markets while broadening its image publicly as a reputable, problem-solving design firm.

Situation Analysis
After a decade of developing a comfortable commercial and residential client base, the firm began in 2005 to take on a broader range of larger-scale educational and institutional design work including religious and federal government (Corps of Engineers) work.

A direction was established to concentrate on local healthcare institutions, public schools, and local, state, and federal government clients. Both the architecture and interior design marketing efforts will concentrate on these markets.

Goals/Strategies/Time Frame

* Become a better-known architecture interior design firm

* Increase interior design services to 30 percent of business volume by January 2007

* Obtain short list/interview for public school project

* Obtain a public school design project

* Obtain a major healthcare interior design project

* Maintain religious design work in Maryland and expand into Delaware

* Maintain and expand Corps of Engineers work

* Concentrate on obtaining open-end contracts with local, state, and federal clients

* Maintain level of new residential as well as additional commissions— in light of the economy and low interest rates

* Expand community college design work

Format of the Marketing Plan

A preliminary marketing plan normally consists of three parts:

* Mission statement

* Situation analysis

* Goals/strategies/time frame

The plan starts with the firm's mission statement. Keep it simple, and under thirty-five words! This paragraph summarizes the who, why, and what you are.

The situation analysis is a written "snapshot" of where the firm is now and where it has been.

The goals/strategies/time frame section deals with just that: your stated goals, the strategies you plan to implement to obtain the goals, and the time frame in which you plan to accomplish your goals. This section provides a benchmark for measuring your success.

SAMPLE MARKETING PLAN

Chart 16 presents a sample marketing plan for a design firm based on the outline presented in this chapter. Use the plan as a guide in developing your new firm's marketing plan.

REALIZING YOUR BRAND

Many start their design firms and are committed to having the firm be an extension of themselves. What does that mean? What is your personal brand? What kind of person are you? Your brand is not what you think it is, rather, it is the perception maintained by others in their relationship with you. This is why it is so important to gain feedback from your future clients. Are your services consistent with who you are? The most important lesson in business is to be who you are. Trust yourself; don't be something or someone you are not. Why live a lie? Be comfortable with yourself, and your clients and employees will be comfortable. Your designs will be comfortable. This process of interaction with others develops relationships. Relationships beget referrals. The cycle continues. Future clients will be attracted to you because of your brand. And if opportunities do not work out, more than likely, the brand wasn't in balance for that prospect. Your brand involves the services that you offer, how you offer them, and what differentiates you from others who offer your services. Be comfortable with your brand. Have it evolve over time. Make sure that you remain true to the brand. As your firm grows, you will have to constantly measure your personal brand with that of your company's. Tracking brand is a very interesting journey.

DESIGN YOUR SUCCESS

Starting and operating a design firm requires flexibility not only from the owner(s) but also from the firm's business and marketing plans. Think simple thoughts, document simple strategies and goals, and provide yourself with a simple framework for success! Read your marketing and business plans at least once a week, if not once a day. Print them out and post them around your office. Remind yourself of who you are and why you are doing what you are doing. If you feel differently about an issue, document the change and continue on with your business. Join the less than 20 percent of design firms that have well–thought-out, documented plans. They are the ones that enjoy success, while the balance sit back and wonder why.

Do yourself a favor. Spend the few hours required to develop the ideas necessary for your plans. Treat this like the schematic design of a project. Keep an open mind. Track your progress. It really can be fun. You will learn a great deal about yourself, and you will have documented the changes and challenges that face you from day to day. Define your brand, and separate yourself from the pack of other design firms. Develop that confidence and culture that is contagious in growth. You will never regret the time spent!

1 2
FEAR, RISK, AND GUILT

"Always do what you are afraid to do."
— RALPH WALDO EMERSON

"Only those who dare to fail greatly can ever achieve greatly."
— ROBERT KENNEDY

"There is no security on this earth, only opportunity."
— DOUGLAS MACARTHUR

"If you listen to your fears, you will die never knowing what a great person you might have been."
— ROBERT H. SCHULLER

No one understands the life, trials, and tribulations of the founding entrepreneurial businessperson. Your family, friends, and clients do not want to hear about your problems, because they don't think that you have any. You have your own business, so you must be successful! You even find it difficult to discuss your feelings with your full-time and part-time employees, because they will probably not understand. Why is it that when I do confide in others, the answers they give me don't make sense? Boy, it is lonely here at the top of my business!

Just as you become comfortable with the "milestone" goal of having your own firm—of not having to listen to anyone else, of being able to run the show—this book comes along and informs you of the hundreds of considerations that come into play, making the decision that much harder and more frightening! Many designers get right to the point of putting on their parachutes, but then—after talking with colleagues or reading a book like this—they refuse to jump out of the airplane because of their fear of failure and rejection.

The reality of it is that all designers who have started their own firms—those who have been successful as well as those who haven't—have experienced the same fear. It is normal. Anyone who says that he or she was confident from the moment of starting out, and has never had a single worry since, is flat-out lying!

Starting and operating a design firm on a daily basis is a challenge. Especially scary is running a business without any formal training or business plan. How many of us had formal business training in our college curriculum or in our former firm? Business acumen is difficult to obtain for many designers. It is much like dealing with the unknown.

WHAT IS FEAR?

Fear is anxiety caused by real or imagined danger or pain. It is apprehension or concern for one's well-being.

Doubt is natural to every human being, young and old, inexperienced and experienced. We all have our limitations. Wiping doubt out of our minds is a technique we all need to learn. Every challenge that we face every day requires a decision. If doubt exists, decisions will not be made, and if they are, the odds are that they will be erroneous.

Many people are fearful about issues that they cannot control. It is human to feel this way. However, in business, there are so many things you can't control that you need to develop a positive mindset.

Determine what you are capable of changing, and do it. Accept what you have no control over changing, and do not try.

Why worry about issues that you cannot control? Suppose you are given the opportunity to present your new firm's qualifications in a personal interview for a major project. Suddenly, the potential client takes ill and asks to reschedule the appointment. Further, the client calls on Friday and promises to call back the following Monday. This event will set many businesspeople "off" in hundreds of ways—to doubting the situation, developing fear, and worrying until the prospect calls.

Some will begin to worry that the client has already made a decision and is not telling the truth. Others, having prepared extensively, will lose their momentum and interest. Still others will wonder if a competitor's interviews went overtime and extremely well.

You must be able to separate your emotional and intellectual feelings on an issue. Sure, emotionally you may be concerned about the client's canceling your interview. However, intellectually you realize you have no control over the situation—so why worry about it? Spend the time you now have open in your afternoon schedule to deal productively with other issues in the firm.

Fear is packaged two ways in life: real fear and imagined fear. The example used above illustrates imagined fear. Real fear is when you need "that" check from your client to make ends meet. You call the client, talk it over, and agree to drive to the client's office to pick up the check personally. Then, when you get there, you discover the client had to leave because of an emergency and didn't sign the check for you. This is the sort of real fear you will experience.

People react to fear because they are afraid of making mistakes, being a failure, and being subject to rejection. Many do not even attempt to take on challenges because of their fear of not succeeding and being subject to ridicule. How many intern designers do you know who are so scared of the professional registration exam that they cannot even find the nerve to take it?

Fear is an emotion that lives with each and every one of us, every hour of every day, and will continue to live with us to our grave. Whether it is passing that test, catching that airplane, getting that job, convincing that client, or having that baby, we will always show concern over events in our lives. Believe it or not, some people have fear of success, and of the potential life that will be associated with their success! They are so comfortable with themselves, they do not want to change for fear that it will make them uncomfortable.

You must learn to view fear positively. Think of fear as the necessary pulse or alternator in your daily life. Every business, from the largest corporation to the smallest one-person design firm, deals with the same concerns and issues, and fear exists in every mind involved. Sure, you can worry about cash flow right along with General Motors. Come to think of it, if you really concentrate, you can imagine that none of your clients will pay you over the next sixty days, and you will go into bankruptcy! What you need to do is take that fear of not being paid (which is imagined fear) and turn it around. Use the emotional energy created to physically call the clients and manage the accounts. Stay on top of it, address it, and channel the fear toward positive action. Remember the extent of the emotional experience of that fear, build upon it, and measure it the next time this encounter occurs. Your experience will remind you of the process you went through; therefore, your fear will be less than when first encountered. Remember the first time you rode your bicycle? Remember the training wheels? The first time your parent or friend "let go" and you rode for the first time without training wheels or that helpful, steady hand that aided you in defying gravity? The same applies to business. Learn by doing. Learn from your mistakes and others' mistakes. Success is the sweet reward for addressing and overcoming your fear(s). Don't feel alone in this difficult part of a firm's development. Talk to others about your fears. You will be amazed at what you hear. Our parents and grandparents helped guide us through life's challenges when we were younger. Why not seek guidance now in an area such as business, in which you have little experience? I have always said, "You can't appreciate the good without experiencing some bad." Life is about encountering good and bad. The successful experience the bad, but are fortunate enough to encounter more good.

Another fear common to all designers is where the next commission will come from. Don't waste time worrying about this issue! Exhibit a positive attitude. Feel confident that the next lead is right around the corner and that you will take it on successfully. For most of us, the next commission will come in out of nowhere, unexpectedly. Some great things happen when you least expect them. You can't be nonchalant about this; but the longer you are in business, you will find that you can count on numerous opportunities to occur from time to time. That is why you always have to "be on" and develop a good, solid reputation. Word will spread positively without you having anything to do with it, thus expanding your network and producing new design opportunities. Remember, it is not what you know, it is who you know that counts in growing a business.

Addressing fear by manipulating it like an alternator in an automobile makes fear work for you. It keeps you alive with a motivating charge, sparking your activity toward success. That pulse, or frequency, is a constant in your day-to-day business life. It is the most important driving force. Think of it as a design challenge. Rarely do we have the entire project designed in the first minute or hour of its life. As a matter of fact, if you were to think of the design process that you would undertake over the next few weeks or months and try to do all of it in a day or two, you would be overwhelmed with fear. But what are we trained to do as designers? We incorporate the steady process of trial and error, step by step, to achieve a successful design composition that satisfies the needs of our client or the aesthetic eye with which we are gifted. When we get behind, the adrenaline kicks in so we can complete the task at hand.

Fear will diminish when you deal with an issue the second time, having learned from the first experience. Also, when you establish inchpebbles, you break down the fear into manageable little pieces, and emotionally you can deal with smaller challenges more easily. It is like getting on that bike for the first time in thirty years. Many of us don't think twice about it, and take it for granted that we will not fall off. And you won't! It is amazing how few of us encounter fear in that experience.

WHAT IS RISK?

Risk is exposure to the chance of injury or loss; it is a hazard or dangerous chance.

Risk as a whole is a disagreeable idea to most people. It is commonly viewed as a negative. Taking risks always implies taking responsibility. People shy away from risk; they prefer to be free from choice and responsibility. They are afraid of failure. They are risk averse. However, there would be no risk without the possibility of failure.

Most people avoid taking risks in the pursuit of life gains; however, they will choose risks to avoid sure losses. The lesson here is that, when faced with certain failure, people do embrace risk; therefore, they are not really averse to risk. They are averse to loss and failure. Resisting risk, and the change it involves, often stems from a fear of appearing stupid. Risk takers, however, usually do things contrary to the norm, and may often be wrong. But being wrong can be part of the process. Didn't your parents tell you to learn from your mistakes?

Learning from the Past

Risk takers point out that risk is a process of trial and error. It is impossible to be perfect; therefore, one will always make mistakes and experience failure. Failure is a far better teacher in life than success, because the lessons learned from failure are more poignant.

In business, very little is predictable. Business can be challenging. It doesn't occur in straight lines, nor is it smooth. Businesspeople have learned over time that to survive in a business enterprise, they must modify and even disrupt old ways of doing things and create new ways. In business, as in life, only change is constant. Many fear change because of uncertainty. Change requires taking risks. Risk taking sometimes results in failure, but only taking risks produces progress and profits.

In business, risk is the agent of change that prevents firms from becoming stagnant. All businesses experience change and risk taking on an hourly and daily basis. Usually, taking risks works, but sometimes it doesn't. The only certainty is that if a company resists change and risks, it will eventually fail.

Think about the older principals in your current or former firm. This comment probably sounds familiar: "That's not the way we do things around here! We know better, because we've been doing design this way for twenty years! We are experienced, so don't challenge it!" One major lesson to learn about taking risks in business is not to base your decisions on past performance. Wake up every day looking forward to the challenge of a new day, and the uncertain challenges that will present themselves to you. Accepting the fact that there will be change is one half of the battle of life. Never be too comfortable. Embrace change, don't fear it. Trust that your alternator will keep the adrenaline flowing to address your challenges. You must be innovative and look into the uncertain future with a confident pair of eyes. Always stay true to your principles, and you will be successful traversing the challenging obstacles of everyday change in your new business world.

Looking to the Future

The art of forecasting for business, like predicting the weather, is not perfect. Nor is being human perfect. As a business owner, you must be flexible in your day-to-day business activity. If something doesn't work, try something else. Developing a flexible approach will help make you take greater risks in the future. Business in the world today, with daily changes in technology, can no longer depend on stable service life cycles. Consider this analogy:

> In the past, running a business was like paddling a canoe on a lake with the water surface like glass. You identified your target (destination), and you glided through the smooth water in a straight line to your goal. The fact was that, if you concentrated and didn't deviate from your course, you would reach your target successfully.
>
> Running a business in today's world is like having the same canoe, but this time you have put into a white water river. The target is visible; however, you will probably have to change course, fight challenging currents, flip upside down, and adjust the direction of your course many times to reach the goal.

Classic entrepreneurs don't take on risk because they love danger. They take on risk because they know that only through risk will they find true value. If entrepreneurs didn't accept risk, enterprise and innovation would not be accomplished. Risk takers create action out of inaction.

Change is unending in business and life. It is uncertain and infinite. Therefore, risk taking must be a continuous process in your daily life. The key to deciding to take on risk is to develop a sense of the degree of a risk. You need to adjust your attitude toward it and learn to live with it. Take on risk intentionally rather than accepting it. Risk taking is an investment in your new firm's future!

WHAT IS GUILT?

Guilt can be described as a feeling of responsibility or remorse for some offense or wrongdoing, whether real or imagined.

To many, guilt is a bad thing in life. Guilt, in my opinion, can be a positive trait if it helps you recognize that you are falling down on the job. It can help you develop good work habits.

One side effect of developing good work habits is developing a business conscience. A business conscience can help you deal with the causes for your guilt. Having that eighth sense, that of a business conscience, will help you manage and guide your firm through the white water of the business environment.

It will aid you in taking risks and in making value judgments and decisions. A conscience will keep you honest and fair and earn you and your firm respect from others. It is a quality that most people admire, and will help you to achieve success through referrals, because clients like you and your firm for what they stand for.

Having and practicing a business conscience can be frustrating and a challenge to your patience. Maintain a positive attitude and keep guilt in check A little guilt is good for a new business. You will be amazed at the impact you will have not only on yourself but on your firm and the people who surround you.

MANAGING RISK, FEAR, AND GUILT

Every day you will be required to manage risk, fear, and guilt. Every decision that you make, from the moment you choose to get up in the morning to that late-night moment you decide to "call it quits for the day," will have risk associated with it. Your experience in similar situations and your ability to deal with fear in unfamiliar areas will determine the degree of your success(es).

Remember, no human is perfect. However, successful people make the "right" decision most of the time. If you face a challenge that tests your experience or throws off your sense of direction, ask a mentor, colleague, or friend to "partner" with you in addressing that necessary decision. Do not avoid making the decision. Unsuccessful people avoid risk, and do not address the issues that face them, by believing that if they ignore the issue, it will simply go away, and their life will return to normal. Nothing can be more untrue in life. Living this way is a lie.

A major criticism leveled at designers is that their major or primary goal in practice and in life is to be "published." Big deal! There is more to life than having your creation documented in a magazine—to be used to dress up your promotional literature, gain accolades from your colleagues, and stroke your ego! You will learn that running a business requires a major set of goals to be addressed on a daily and hourly basis. Getting published and receiving testimonies are fine goals, but to achieve them will require you to address numerous other challenges to get there. Think of it this way: If you only focus on getting published, and you do not manage your marketing or financial responsibilities, you may not have that other, new design commission to work on while the original project is being published, let alone the cash necessary to live on during this process.

The best way to manage fear, risk, and guilt is to set goals and remain focused on them. The best way to address them is to understand and embrace the balance that it is necessary to maintain with all of them to achieve your successes. Success is built on good work habits, routines, and goals.

You will find it easier to handle the challenges surrounding your new firm if you balance priorities and set routines. The following are some observations that should help guide you on a daily basis:

1. Your new firm isn't the only entity in your life. Family, friends, and social life are just as important! Try to develop a balance among all your interests.

2. Develop great health standards. Work out to address stress, eat well to maintain good nutrition—the necessary fuel you will need to have a clear mind to take on the daily challenges.

3. Get organized and set goals—small, medium, and large.

4. Normalize your work habits:

   ◆ Arrive at your office every morning at the same time.

   ◆ Eat breakfast every morning.

   ◆ Attempt to eat lunch at the same time every day.

   ◆ Plan the use of your practice's prime time (8:00 A.M. to 5:00 P.M.) with great care; this is the normal time that clients, vendors, and other businesses operate.

5. Take at least one day of the week off to recharge your batteries. Do something other than your practice. It is important to have and engage in other hobbies, such as cooking, wine, cycling, hiking, travel. Do something active, not passive like watching TV or playing computer games. Your body needs to be active to assist your mind.

6. Limit your work hours to a maximum sixteen hour workday, or eighty hours per week, during your initial start-up phase.

7. Get a reasonable amount of sleep each night. Be true to yourself. Each of us is built differently; therefore we need different amounts of rest to feel refreshed.

8. Pace yourself. Set realistic goals to achieve each day. Organize your day into three or four units of four hours. If you underestimate your efforts, learn from your estimations, do the work, and move on with other goals. Don't lose sight of your daily goals.

9. Plan the events of each new workweek on Sunday evening. Don't wait until Monday morning. Few are fortunate to have all senses and faculties on the morning of the first day of the week. Take some time on Sunday to review what you accomplished the previous week, and what needs to be addressed in the week ahead. It is so healthy to do this. This exercise will help you address the stress in your life, as well as measure your progress.

10. Start Monday morning with the proper attitude—for your benefit as well as for those who work with you.

11. Set appointments with yourself to study and address administrative, financial, marketing, and other business issues. As a designer, it is tempting to want to design as much of the time as possible. Learn that this is not a reality in running a design business. Make a commitment to yourself to address the necessary issues on a regular basis by setting up, and keeping, appointments to deal with them. Be true to yourself. This is another way to measure your progress.

12. Market, market, market!

13. Perform as many production-oriented tasks outside of prime business hours (8:00 A.M. to 5:00 P.M.) as possible. Remember, you need quality time to focus on getting the production work complete. After prime hours can be a quiet time to focus on the important decisions that you are ultimately liable for. Spend your prime hours meeting and networking with others, and doing marketing. Figure out what time of day you are at your best for designing and other activities. Commit yourself to doing those activities during those time frames.

14. Be available to everyone via phone or e-mail during the prime time hours of the business day, bar none. If you are unavailable, develop a habit of returning calls either that morning, or afternoon, no longer than one business day later.

15. Take a "quiet hour" in the evening to reflect on lessons learned that day. Avoid the phone and e-mail, and recharge your batteries for just a little time to help separate yourself from others.

Once you start your firm, you will see how easy it is to work sixteen to twenty hours per day! You don't physically have to be at the office or with a client to be working. Your mind will start working when you awake in the morning, while you take your shower, on the commute to the office, through lunch, on the commute to a meeting, on the way home, during and after dinner, and even as you lie in bed awaiting sleep.

If you allow yourself to become a time clock, you will be successful, but successful in only one aspect of life: time management. There is more to life than work, career, and profession! Truly successful entrepreneurial designers are able to develop a critical balance among business, family, friends, and profession. Developing and maintaining that balance will provide a richer, healthier, and more fulfilling life.

REFINING YOUR DAILY ROUTINE

In your daily routine, it is important to establish small, obtainable goals—the inchpebbles referred to throughout this book Simple goals, to obtain on a daily basis, may include not only waking up at 6:00 A.M. but getting out of bed at 6:00 A.M.! Simple goals in business include starting your day consistently at 8:00 A.M., making two marketing cold calls per day, designing your projects in the morning when you are rested and fresh, and conducting administrative and marketing functions in the afternoon when most of your clients are in their offices, out of meetings, and available to communicate with. Work on your construction documents and other production tools in the afternoon and evening, when your time can be focused without much interruption. Another goal may be to work Monday through Thursday from 8:00 A.M. to 9:00 P.M., and Saturday mornings only, due to your other interests on Saturday afternoons and Sundays. Long-range goals—milestones in the journey to success—are visionary and need to be the sum of many inchpebbles.

Daily routines are important because they develop momentum and a work ethic to get your tasks completed. Having a daily routine will become predictable and respected by others, especially the important ones: your clients. I have a few clients who know that if they really need to speak with me, I am commuting to my office from 6:30 A.M. to 7:00 A.M. every day. They will call me on my cell phone on a regular basis. It is my decision to take the call by reviewing caller ID, but it is my choice, and my clients feel value in knowing that it is a quiet time and I am available solely for their needs. It is a win-win situation, because I can be of value and service before the 8:00 A.M. prime time "starting bell" rings.

Having a daily routine really helps get your tasks completed in a timely fashion. Many of my colleagues love to arrive at their office between 6:30 A.M. and 7:00 A.M., because the phone call traffic is quiet, and they can catch up on their e-mails and other important planning issues, maybe design work or producing "red-line markups" for the production staff to incorporate in their production work that day. Do whatever it takes to stay ahead of the demands of your schedule, your family, clients' expectations, your hobbies, etc. If you get up when the morning alarm goes off, whatever time you choose, and you get out of bed and on with your routine, you improve the chances of having a great day.

A word of caution for those of you who dislike routines because of their implied structure or predictability: As a businessperson, you will be in for many challenges in your business career. Many designers prefer sleeping in late, arriving to the studio well after the 8:00 A.M. start time, and remaining very late in the evening—sometimes well after midnight, well into the next day. They will say that they are putting in the same effort and time necessary to work on their projects, and on "their terms and time." They may be correct on that point; however, in our business world, there are important people called contractors and clients. Most contractors start their days very early in the morning, some as early as 6:00 A.M. By the time the designers arrive at 10:00 A.M., the contractor has performed half a day of work! The designer has not been available for questions or assistance during any of that time. Those designer types may say that it does not concern them, that in those cases, it is the contractor's issue that they begin their workday on their own terms.

This is a very selfish position to take. As designers, we are in a career to assist others; it is not about us. We should be considerate of others and perform what it takes to address their needs in a timely fashion, whatever time that may mean.

Establishing a routine is like setting a deadline everyday for yourself. It is a commitment for excellence and being of value to yourself and others. As for deadlines, set a deadline for every task that you assign yourself! When you receive a commission for a project, establish a schedule and determine the various deadlines needed to accomplish work that meets your client's expectations. You will be amazed at how impressed clients will be with your sense of care and organization if you state, after accepting a commission, that you would like to discuss the target dates for all the project's phases or tasks and tentatively commit your time and theirs to those specific dates. Few in today's world give the impression of organization. Having the willingness and ability to plan ahead, and provide a measured way to address and resolve your client's needs, has unprecedented value in the business marketplace.

Many clients will say, "Can you really commit to meeting with me on every fourth Wednesday at 7:00 P.M.? I am not sure that I can make that commitment." This is a great position to be in as their designer. You have the ability and leadership style that will be respected. You may reply "In order for me to be an effective steward of your project and design fee, I have to commit to a structure of project management, and establish deadlines to be effective, before we begin our journey. Those deadline dates may be subject to change; however, we will begin our work with an understanding."

The ability to make time commitments and to keep them will be one of the major assets that differentiates you from your competition. I have utilized this mindset for twenty-five years, and my personal and firm's successes have far exceeded any that I imagined the day that I decided to start my firm. Remember, to others, perception is reality. If you appear confident and experienced due to your commitment and organizational structural skills, all the better. You will be respected and, most importantly, be of value and be referred to others for more design work, because of your being different—in other words, better—than the rest. Isn't that what it is all about?

Being deadline-oriented makes you appear and become disciplined. You will be more productive and better organized; you will appear to be more logical. Most important, you will radiate accountability, responsibility, and success! Clients appreciate these qualities in designers and consultants, because it assures them that they have made a right decision, and it makes them look good.

THE VALUE OF A TIME MANAGEMENT SYSTEM

The simplest, most fundamental thing you can do first is to purchase a time management system to help you organize your time and daily "things to do" list. Further, this device will give you a method to schedule periodic reviews, deadlines, and anniversaries and to record long-range ideas and observations.

Many designers utilize a handwritten data entry system such as a "daytimer" or "week at a glance" system to assist them in keeping track of their life as well as their company's. Another benefit of keeping such a daily diary is that it gives you a detailed record of your day-to-day activity to look back on and learn from—and then to set new goals based on your experiences. It also provides a time management tool to measure your time spent on projects for billing purposes and profit management.

Many designers utilize a PC-based software time management calendar program, such as Microsoft Outlook, for their needs. Being PC-based, whether you use your desktop or a laptop, it can be a very dependable system. For many, having to turn on a computer to access their schedule data becomes inconvenient. Many begin to print out their schedules and address books on paper for easier reference.

Another popular technological advancement is the PDA or personal data assistant—a calculator-sized microprocessor that records your schedule and activities. Having made its debut a number of years ago, this device has become indispensable to many businesspeople. This hardware device is interfaced with a PC for convenience and expandability of data storage. Information can be shared with your assistant's, colleague's, or spouse's PC so that your office also has your schedule and can print out a hard copy as backup if necessary.

Many PDAs on the market today also incorporate your cell phone and e-mail needs, such as the BlackBerry or Palm Treo. Most of the tools that you need in organizing your business needs are all in one handheld device. You can be away from your studio or office and still be connected with your staff, clients, and contractors, making these devices indispensable.

Probably, the most valuable attribute of the PDA is that it is one resource that stores all of your calendar, address, tasks-to-do, and general information data that you need in one handheld device. It is backed up on your PC, and should you lose it or break it, the information is retrievable. Also, all the data is archivable. Therefore, all your appointments are documented for as long as you utilize the system. This has great value when you have to research your time spent on a project in the distant past. The PDA is a great business tool. As with technology in general, PDAs evolve every day, and render those created just a few months or a year ago obsolete.

In order to be successful in operating your business, you will need to meet more and greater challenges every day. Learn not to depend on your memory for all scheduled events. Few people have the ability to retain so much information. Remember the idea of scheduled events, and let your written diary or computer organizer retain the details. Learn to depend on it.

Your time management system is your best friend in planning the future and in documenting a present that is soon to be the past. It can be not only a repository of data, but also a planning tool from which to learn. It is a system of measurement and accountability. If you are effective and consistent with good recording habits, your time management system will help you achieve success much quicker than you ever imagined.

THERE ARE ONLY 168 HOURS IN A WEEK!

Manage your time. Next to your ideas and creativity, it is the most sacred commodity in business. Remember, there are only 168 hours in a week. That's all; there is no chance of adding any more!

Let's be analytical about this. Think about those 168 hours. Most of us need an average of seven hours of sleep per day (forty-nine hours per week, or 28 percent of our time!) Another forty hours (33 percent) are prime business hours: Monday through Friday, 8:00 A.M. to 5:00 P.M.

The secret of success is how you manage the remaining seventy-nine hours.

In your first year of business, you may feel that it is necessary to work at least eighty hours per week, which leaves a precious thirty-nine hours to commute, eat, work around the house, and relax! Is that enough? These time constraints make it essential to maintain a balance among the business, personal, professional, and family requirements in your life. Learn not to be emotional and develop workaholic traits. Look at your 168 hours objectively at first, then subjectively in planning them. You will learn that each one is precious. Never in your life has every single hour of every single week been so important!

The interesting thing is that if you spend too much time in one area of your life, the other areas begin to suffer. Stress and discontent result. Learn to read the signs in your family, friends, and colleagues, and in yourself! Your relationships and health can be at risk if you do not effectively manage your life and time, and give each their fair due. No one wants to be treated as important only part of the time. You need to "partner" the various areas of your life and develop a way of getting them to work in concert with one another. No one area is more important than another. All are equal in value because they are interdependent. Clients depend on your business, the business depends on you, and your family depends on you, your business, and your clients. It all goes round and round! Maintaining this balance is one of the most important exercises in life to obtaining and maintaining true happiness.

MAINTAIN A CRITICAL BALANCE

Goal setting is an ongoing exercise. As in your design practice, set the easy, obtainable goals first to gain confidence and develop momentum. This will help you set and obtain the more complex goals later.

Challenge yourself! Set goals, both milestones and inchpebbles, and you will be amazed at how quickly you obtain results. Use time management techniques to help maintain a critical balance among the various areas of your life (family, friends, business, profession, community) and to partner them into one concerted effort toward success.

Establishing a routine is probably the best way to implement a goal-oriented personal lifestyle.

The truth of the matter is that you start your firm each and every day that you are in business. Every day brings a different scope of challenges to take on. Life is about change. Your new firm will change each and every day; learn to accept and understand this. Starting each day is fun.

Manage fear, risk, and guilt (your business conscience) by dealing successfully with inchpebbles, and evaluate your progress in quarterly and annual reviews. You will be surprised at how taking the time to study past facts and events will give you the confidence and experience you need to meet future challenges head on.

13
SUCCESS

"Success is not so much what you are, as what you appear to be."
—ANONYMOUS

"You always pass failure on the way to success."
—MICKEY ROONEY

"There are no secrets to success. It is the result of preparation, hard work, and learning from failure."
—COLIN POWELL

"The most important single ingredient in the formula of success is knowing how to get along with people."
—THEODORE ROOSEVELT

"Try not to become a man of success, but rather try to become a man of value."
—ALBERT EINSTEIN

"I don't know the key to success, but the key to failure is trying to please everybody."
—BILL COSBY

I'll never forget getting that first large design contract. My goal in my first year was to have $30,000 a year under contract for total revenue. The new project called for performing construction administration *services for only seven months and was valued at $6,000! Imagine, this one contract was 20 percent of my yearly goal, and it came into my life out of nowhere! That night, my wife and I celebrated with a major dinner and an incredible bottle of wine. Now that made starting my new firm all worthwhile!*

Seeing my name on my personal checks throughout college was no big deal. However, the first time I prepared and cut a check with my new firm's name on it was a significant event in my life! I thought to myself, "Aren't this check and the company name impressive? This check has value, it is important, and am I ever impressed!" I first felt pride of ownership when I left my new office on my first day of business. When I closed the door behind me, I felt the most incredible sense of accomplishment, like none that I have ever experienced.

The reality of the actual start-up of my firm really didn't hit me until the first time the telephone rang, and I had to answer it. When I answered it with the new firm name, it took some courage and was awkward, but once I uttered the name, I had an instant moment of pride and accomplishment.

WHAT IS SUCCESS?

Success is having a favorable result (wealth, fame, or any other outcome) turn out the way it was hoped for.

In business, both success and excellence tend to be measured in ways that can be quantified, i.e., cash flow, quarterly revenue and profit, the balance sheet and profit/loss statement comparing this year to last year, design awards, community recognition, etc. Others have said that success is measured over time. In design, however, success is not so clearly defined, because there is no single definition of it and there is no one formula for achieving it. It has been said by many a designer that "my next design will be my best," building and learning from their last design experience. If that were the case for design success, would any client ever retain our services? I believe that, as designers, we strive for excellence in each and every design to meet and exceed the expectations and needs of the owner.

The target of goal setting, whether inchpebbles or milestones, is success.

Success begins with the proper attitude, and starts with you! Developing a "victorious" attitude assumes from the very beginning that, in all you do, you are going to come out on top. Try it! From the moment that you awake in the morning until you complete that last design decision late at night, be confident and communicate it to others through your body language, attitude, and verbal communications.

Isn't it human nature to have ups and downs? How can you be "up" all day? The answer lies in how you approach your challenges and act or react when encountering others. Be a salesperson all day. When you talk to your client, banker, or lawyer, have an upbeat, confident, victorious attitude. Be assured. Confidence is catching! When people encounter someone who exhibits the above characteristics, they believe that the person is successful and want to associate themselves with that person. Think about it. People want to deal with successful people. This is why some are attracted to celebrities, and others are attracted to a successful person's expertise.

Clients want to deal with successful design firms and their principals because they want to get value for their money and design product. Dealing with a successful designer brings notoriety and peace of mind that the professional is experienced, creative, responsible, and accountable and will design a building that meets the client's expectations.

Your banker wants to deal with a successful designer for two obvious reasons. First, if you have been granted a loan from the bank, your banker wants you to succeed so you can pay back the principal and, most important, the interest on the loan. That is one of the reasons banks exist: to make money on business. Your success also makes your lender look good to their bank leadership, proving that you are a reasonable risk, providing a reasonable return on the bank's money. He or she will be viewed as being able to bring in a quality customer to whom the bank can be of service while making a profit. Second, your banker wants you to succeed because chances are that if you design well and service clients well, your firm will grow and prosper and have more money needs. Guess who has all the money for your needs?

Your attorney wants you to be successful so that he or she won't have to represent you in court over any issue. The attorney would rather help you develop and/or review contracts and form the business, and give you advice on day-to-day operations and how the law affects your decisions. A good client for an attorney may start small as a sole proprietor and grow into a partnership or corporation. There is plenty of work for the lawyer to do in refining your forms of business and reviewing your leases as you shift to new quarters because your spatial needs have increased due to new employees and equipment. Your attorney is also a networking opportunity. Once your attorney gets the sense that you are accountable, responsible, and creative, he may refer new business (his clients and contacts) to you.

Your accountant wants you to be successful because it is her or his job to document your business activity and give you advice on present and future challenges. Accountants are wizards with numbers. They can make an average year look great! They can help assist you in understanding how your quarter, or year, was unsuccessful so that you can better identify and address your company's needs. As your business becomes more and more successful, you will need more services from your accountant. In the beginning, the accountant may generate your simple income statement and balance sheets, and probably your initial tax returns. Later on, he or she will develop trial statements for accounting review and approval before submission to your lender. Your accountant understands the numbers and ratios of a successful, profitable business. He or she can assist you in evaluating the business sense of a new lease that you feel is the next step in occupancy for your successful firm. Listen to your accountant's advice. This person deals with successes and failures every day with other customers.

The longer you are in business, the more challenges you will encounter and the more experience you will gain. Successful designers are not just the ones who get published in the magazines. "Creativity" is a buzz word in the design business that is measured, by many, by the ability and/or potential to design aesthetically pleasing compositions, resulting in an artful success. From my perspective, this is only one variable of success in the design firm equation of business. "Being creative" means so much more than producing aesthetically pleasing projects. It can mean that you created the right design to address your client's budget, or their business performance goals. Don't let the "creative" label get in the way of your successes.

Successful principals are also those individuals whose firms have survived—staying in business for one, two, three, four, or more years. Sure, many designers speak negatively about their experiences—they do not make much money, they work too hard. That is their problem. One of the things that inspired me to write this book was my desire to help aspiring businesspeople avoid that trap. The fact of the matter is that most of our colleagues do a poor job of running their firms. They don't have the formal business training or the initiative to plan. They want to be designers first, designing design, and let the business fall as it may. And sadly, many do not care or want to learn the business skills necessary to produce a successful, profitable business. To them, their profit is the "great design" they produce. What they fail to understand, and will hopefully learn, is that it takes more than a creative mind producing pleasing or trendy aesthetics to be successful. Their definition of business "profit" is the money left over at the end of the year. They will not be in business very long. They will eventually either take on another partner who possesses business acumen, or perish.

INGREDIENTS FOR ENTREPRENEURIAL SUCCESS

Before you start your firm, know yourself. You need to exploit your strengths and overcome your weaknesses to obtain success. If you are good in design, take that for granted and concentrate on your administration, production, marketing, and financial skills. Many firms are founded with at least two, or maybe three to four, partners each wanting to design, but each one also specializing in one of the other four areas of the practice. Set your inchpebble and milestone goals, achieve them, and be successful! Most importantly, if you have partners, make sure that you communicate your needs and expectations for the good of the organization as well as for each other. Too many times individuals form a business entity not understanding or accepting each other's strengths and weaknesses, and they end up with many unexpected challenges and fail.

The following are essential ingredients for entrepreneurial success.

1. Successful designers have clear, definable goals. Always. Designers who wander here and there usually do not succeed. Stay on course to achieve your goals. Goals are the "mind" of your new venture.

2. All of us care passionately about our designs, but you will now have to care passionately about your new firm and your service to your clients. You need to be so passionate about your new entity and its outcomes that it will strain your relationship with friends and family

because they will grow tired of hearing about it. Passion is the heart of your new enterprise.

3. As a designer, you must persevere. Listen to that small, stubborn voice that says, "I'm not going to give up. I don't care what you say or think!" Be tenacious and committed to your new venture. This is the strength and muscle behind your new business.

4. You need to be organized and prepared every day. This book has attempted to give you some idea of what you will encounter. Do your homework! Diminish the risk. Organization is the skeleton or structure of your new enterprise.

5. You must maintain perspective. This is what will keep you from going insane during the entire process. When you are afraid of failure, perspective will remind you that failure isn't fatal, and the business is not the only variable in your life. Other things matter as well. Perspective will also keep you from getting a swelled head if you are successful. Perspective is achieved by measurement of activity and experience. Be honest with yourself, and trust your genuine thoughts on your position and status at the time of review.

6. You need to perform. Your dreams and vision are very important when you own your own firm; however, they do not take the place of getting the job done! As a designer, you have to motivate yourself to do the work—because there is no boss over you. You are it! As I say every day when I go to work, "Make it happen." I have been thinking this thought many times a day over the more than twenty-five–year journey of success of my firm.

7. You must have presence! In business, presence is the ability to hold clients' attention when you are with them and be remembered by them when you are not.

THE JOURNEY CONTINUES . . .

Remember that success is not a destination, it is a journey.

It is all a matter of perspective. You are a success every day, it just depends upon your point of view. Success breeds success. Successful people tend to make things happen with their lives, and associate themselves with other successful people. Some success is about luck, and other success is about knowing the right people. As the saying goes, "it is not what you know, but who you know."

Being successful is not just about being creative or designing one great aesthetic project. It is more than just design. Success is a way of life. It is about how you behave, how you think, and who you choose to associate with. Success can be contagious. Think about it. Always be aware of the potential negative, but focus on the positive and trust yourself when you are being genuine with yourself. This is the mindset of the successful.

From the moment you were born, you have been on your life journey. Now, having started your new business, you have added a very interesting variable into your life equation. You know about your past, and you are somewhat aware of your present; now what exactly lies out there in the future?

14

THE FUTURE

"With high hope for the future, no prediction is ventured."
—ABRAHAM LINCOLN

"I never think of the future. It comes soon enough."
—ALBERT EINSTEIN

"The only thing we know about the future is that it will be different."
—PETER F. DRUCKER

"The future starts today, not tomorrow."
—POPE JOHN PAUL II

After my first year in practice, my wife and I took a trip to Greece to visit friends and see the beginnings of Western architecture. Having lived with myself for a year, with sixteen-hour days six days a week, completely saturated with my business, I will never forget the most humbling experience of my entire life. There I was, standing on the Acropolis, thinking the entire world was centered back in the office that I had left 7,500 miles behind. Not one person within one hundred feet of me was speaking English, and no one could have cared less that I was an architect with the most important practice in the world 7,500 miles away! That really put my life, business, and future in perspective.

Many of you will hear: "Darling, you are working so many hours overtime. I haven't seen much of you, and the kids have forgotten who you are! You are wearing yourself down, and I worry about you. Working too hard can be unhealthy, and if you drop dead, I will kill you."

Now that you have started on your new adventure in life, you can expect to encounter the ultimate challenges and thrills associated with developing, cultivating, and growing a new business enterprise: *your design firm!* You have embarked upon the most rewarding and most frustrating exercise of your life. Maintaining a balance in the firm's organization and operation while being profitable is a difficult challenge.

As a firm owner, you will face different challenges every minute, every hour, every day, every month, and every year! You will encounter several changes in your personal life, and several business cycles during your lifetime. Risk, change, fear, and success run hand in hand for the business owner in all these aspects of balance.

THE THREE FACES OF OWNERSHIP

Thousands of designers leave the companies they work for each year in order to start their own firms. Most of them have a fuzzy idea (blurred vision) of growing their infant practice into a thriving, well-recognized firm. Growth is almost always a goal for designers. Should you decide that growth is for you and your firm, you can expect to experience the following role changes in the future:

First person	Owner/founder
Second person	Owner/manager
Third person	Chief executive officer

First Person. Owner/Founder

Once you have started your firm, you are the owner and totally responsible for its success. You do it all. You certainly have pride in yourself and your design product, and you feel independent. You provide a high level of personalized service to your clients since you control and do all of the design and production.

As we have discussed, however, there are limitations on you and your new start-up firm if you do not grow. First of all, there is not enough of "you" to go around once you take on multiple projects. Further, if you have no staff, there is no backup. Frustration may set in because you will feel like you are running the business more than designing, and are out of control of your destiny.

You have reached a decision point. Should you grow? Do you take on one or more partners or add staff? Some, the minority, will make a positive, definitive decision to limit the amount of business that they can handle and not address growth. They are comfortable and confident that they alone will control their destiny, one project at a time. They are content in this decision. It takes a certain mindset and culture to make this decision and commitment. The secret to this approach is to limit and schedule your potential business in such a way that your self-proclaimed work schedule of thirty, forty, fifty, sixty, seventy, or eighty hours per week will allow you to achieve your deadlines alone, without getting behind, so that you can meet or exceed your clients' expectations. In this situation, you really need to know yourself and what your capabilities are. Few are gifted in all aspects of their professional career. In this case, however, you need to be proficient in all aspects. There is no one else there to lean on. Also, for many, it is very difficult to have the will power and to say no to business opportunities, in spite of your self-imposed, limited schedule. Few potential clients will want to wait a period of time, waiting for you to complete your current workload commitment, for you to serve and address their design needs. It can be a struggle for some. For others, it is the only way of life that they know. They cannot entrust, delegate, or work with other staff.

Another point about the classic sole proprietor is that, for most, income may be limited to a certain level due to the amount of time they can commit and produce for their firm. The mindset in the design professions is to not associate income with time of service, but with the value of the service. In other words, these designers feel that their income should not be based only upon the 2,000 to 3,000 billable hours they generate per year. They feel their product is worth more that the time it takes to produce it, and that the client should appreciate that. This mindset is logical and certainly understandable, but in the business marketplace, most client prospects fail to understand this about professional services.

However, remaining a sole proprietorship is certainly one path a business can take.

If you elect to grow, you enter the next stage of your individual business development: the second person.

Second Person. Owner/Manager

If you felt frustrated during your first-person experience, you can welcome an entire new set of rules and issues to add to your frustration in this next phase! Since you decided that there is not enough of you to go around, you have added a partner or staff. Now you must learn to manage not only yourself and the firm, but other people! As a designer, you were trained to design, not manage firms and people. You have to manage your people by forcing them all to think like you, because everyone who retains your services wants *you*, right? Wrong! You must develop people skills and effectively manage your staff or partner to turn out a consistent, successful design product.

Consider the story of a talented carpenter's apprentice who, once qualified, left the firm and started his own carpentry subcontracting company. He framed a house, then another, and another, and the word got out that this particular carpenter was good, very good. Soon he had more projects than he knew what to do with! He had to make a decision: to turn work down or to hire carpenters who, in his view, were not as good as he was and then assume a new role of monitoring their work and producing a consistent product. The great carpenter became a great manager.

This is a very important stage in your professional career. Many design professionals have difficulty managing others. They can manage clients and projects, but not employees. You need to decide whether you can delegate the responsibility necessary to grow. Growth isn't for everyone. Many professionals experience unsuccessful growth because they cannot delegate authority well or cannot share control and ownership well. As a result, they lose good, experienced staff.

This second-person stage can go on for the rest of your career. However, should you decide to seek the next plateau, you will be the manager of managers in your firm, or the chief executive officer.

Third Person. Chief Executive Officer

At the third-person stage in your career, you will focus on the management of the business and make decisions about the firm's direction, consider branch offices and mergers, and think about expanding the firm to other design disciplines.

Few designers get to this stage of a business since their firms are generally smaller operations, with a staff of ten or less. Interestingly, the more staff and managers you control, the more income you will command.

You will most probably encounter the first- and second-person experiences within the first few years of your new firm. The third-person experience is saved for the select few who are cut out for that particular challenge. Please note that it is possible to not know where your journey will take you. You may have forethoughts of running a smaller-sized firm, but life may present opportunities that will test your abilities and senses. Whatever level of business you end up in, be sure to trust yourself, and make sure that you are meeting your mission in life. Do not take on new business for growth if you are uncomfortable. Don't grow to impress others. Nothing can be worse than growing for the wrong reasons. This third phase is primarily for those designers who have business acumen and are driven by the income side of the practice. That is not to say that they are good or great designers; however, their purpose or mission may be to enhance the quality of life for many other designers through their leadership skills, affecting the lives of many others with their work product. The bottom line is to live each day for what it brings you, and address each and every challenge in your own way.

BUSINESS LIFE CYCLES

Like people, firms age. As newborns they enter an introductory stage. As adolescents, a growth stage. As adults, a maturity stage. And if careful planning isn't exercised, they enter a decline stage leading to their demise. These are the life-cycle stages that the majority of businesses experience.

Introductory Stage

The introductory stage, like infancy, is the riskiest of the four. If your commissions are viable, and if you manage your firm's vital signs well and have a little luck, at the end of your first year in business you will be "in the black" financially rather than "in the red." If you continue to monitor the vital signs and keep tight reins on your firm's spending, you will maintain profitability month to month, and develop the necessary cash to fuel your firm's growth. As business volume grows, you will gradually need part-time help and eventually full-time employees.

Many have asked, over time, "How does one know when to add staff to the firm?" The simplest way to determine staff need is this: Turn your contracted effort (your design contract dollar values) into man-hour data for each and every phase of the project. Apply this data to deadline dates, determining how many man hours are required per week to get the work done to meet the deadline. This data should be tracked over a thirteen-week calendar on a computer spreadsheet program that you can create yourself, the Man-hour Status Spreadsheet. You can track all of your active projects concurrently, by listing the projects in the first column and summarizing the contracted effort in time, each week over the thirteen-week time frame in the adjacent thirteen columns. All time is summarized on the bottom line to track the present and upcoming man-hour needs for your firm.

Once you accept more work than you are willing to do yourself, as measured in the spreadsheet, this tool will begin to communicate a need for part-time or full-time staff. For example: Let's say that you are willing to work approximately seventy-five hours per week for the first year, and fifty hours are for design/production time, fifteen are for marketing, and ten are for administrative efforts. Your first contract fee for just the design portion of the project is $30,000. Your schedule requires you to complete the design in three months. Figuring your average hourly rate at $100.00 per hour, your contract has three hundred hours of time for you to do the design work. In a three-month time frame, that works out to one hundred hours per month or twenty-five hours per week. You still have twenty-five hours a week to spend time doing other design/production tasks for the firm. Should you decide to do the project quicker, you could commit forty hours of your time, and do the project in approximately seven weeks' time. Once you add one or two more projects and they require more than fifty hours per week of design/production effort, you need additional staff or you will spend more time than you have allotted for design to do the work. Obviously, once your design/production efforts increase to over eighty hours a week, you need another staff person to assist. Tracking that 80 + hour-per-week contractual commitment with your clients on the spreadsheet depicts the backlog of work to sustain your new staff over a period of time. This is one of the most important tools you can develop and utilize in maintaining and measuring balance in your life. Conversely, when the staff hours exceed those projected by your contract's financial and deadline parameters, you may have to consider reducing staff or engage them to do more of the work faster for the client. These are unsettling challenges, but the Man-hour Status Spreadsheet is a great forecaster for manpower needs for the entire business quarter. This spreadsheet is your "magic ball" looking into the near future.

Use common sense and set your sights on a goal to add staff, whether administrative or technical, during the first year. Keep ploughing your profits back into the firm's operations to maintain a steady climb. You will be surprised at the results if you focus on your vision, even if you are attempting to "just survive."

There is a fine line between growth and survival during the first few years of your new firm. Remember, there is no magic formula to help you make the transition between the introductory stage and the growth stage. The Man-hour Status Spreadsheet will act as your conscience through this journey. With every new project, translate the fee into measured effort over a time frame of deadlines to develop an accurate measurement of your future man-hour efforts. Remain focused and true to your firm by constant attention and investment, and before you know it you will be in the growth stage.

Growth Stage

As in every business, if you are a good designer, a good person, or an accountable business person, it will not take long for the word to spread, and you will begin to receive and accept multiple commissions. The sheer number of projects to be handled, along with the deadlines imposed to get work done, will force you to consider delegating some tasks to others.

Deciding to Grow. This is a critical time in your firm's life. You must make the decision to grow or not. By now, you probably have learned more about yourself than at any other time in your life. Can you manage others? Do you want to do it all? Can you delegate to others? Do you want to delegate? If you choose growth, start slowly. Don't let your ego get in the way and hire more staff than you really need. Use the Man-hour Status Spreadsheet to guide your staffing needs. Usually, once you get to two or three staff, you may develop the need for part-time administrative support to do word processing or bookkeeping. A rule of thumb for administrative staff is one full-time admin staff for every five to seven full-time professional staff positions. Growth can also involve a new partner or a new discipline for your new firm. Be entrepreneurial and genuine with yourself and others, and take on a calculated risk for a predetermined period of time. Not all ventures are successful in time. If something looks great, but then it doesn't provide a return on your investment in a reasonable period of time, consider changing its course or

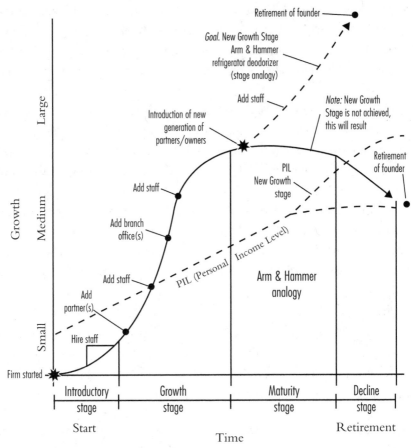

Design Firm Business Cycles

terminating it. Why create a financial drain for your company? You are in business to make money, not lose it. You are in practice to make great design, not bad design.

The Future. Remember, one person *can* do it all—but only by limiting intake and delivery. It is difficult to say no when potential clients show interest in you, providing you with a great opportunity to design a project for them. If you know yourself well and are sure you cannot say no, then growth is in your future. If you can say no, balance your schedule and keep demand in line with what it takes to maintain your own reputation. Then you can do it alone, with only yourself to criticize. This is the goal of many designers. However, you can also hire staff to help you design your projects in the good times, releasing them if necessary when the bad times come. You will still be around to do the work.

Growth requires cash, so invest your profits back into the firm to add new equipment and staff. Banks love firms that grow, because growth devours cash! And guess who has the cash if your firm doesn't? When a firm experiences growth, profits are usually excellent, expansion begins, and issues such as relocation, upgrading firm image, and acquisitions and mergers become considerations.

One of the ways to address growth is by monitoring your firm's vital signs. When you are bringing in more business than you can possibly handle by yourself, it is time to get some design assistance. As noted in chapter 12, there are only 168 hours in a week. You can physically work only so many hours. The workload will determine if your new assistant needs to be full or part time. Starting a person on a part-time basis is less risky. You won't have to provide benefits and other incentives as you would for a full-time employee. Many designers with full-time employment elsewhere are looking for "a few extra bucks" and will be happy to assist you on weekends or evenings. Make sure that you track and measure your part-time employees' efforts to ensure your firm's profitability. Your part-time staff may be well-intentioned but not effective. This relationship requires a lot of trust from both parties. This is a great first "baby-step" in growing your company. You will be amazed at how this will help your business. First off, you will have more time to market and monitor your firm's business. You will also have someone else to share your challenges with. Who knows? Maybe the part-time person is more skilled at some tasks than you are and will be more effective, yielding a better profit for the company. This is what successful enterprise is all about, being able to maintain a personal balance and increasing your firm's profitability. In business, this is referred to as "leverage." You are leveraging the skills of others to allow you to be focused on your "highest and best" use for the company. Leveraging staff requires effective delegation. Delegation requires effective management. It is the continuum in the growth phase of a business.

The same holds true for the administrative and accounting functions of the firm. If you are processing all the correspondence and specifications, as well as handling all the bills and invoices, at some point you will become overwhelmed with the financial administrative needs of the business. These tasks can be done very cost-effectively by computer, and by others. You were not trained as a designer to do these tasks.

The biggest bridge to cross as a designer facing growth is delegation. When do you let go and allow another to do the task? Remember, you are ultimately in charge and accountable. But you cannot do everything! You must give good instructions to those who will be supporting you. There is nothing wrong with delegating responsibility to others to leverage your abilities. Who knows? You may learn that someone else may do something better than you can. Imagine that. This bridge crosses from self management to the management of others. This is a very important and interesting bridge to cross in your journey. You will never learn more about people and yourself than you will in crossing this bridge.

Planning for Growth. To understand business and achieve success in growth, you must understand the difference between controlled and explosive growth.

Controlled growth is the planned, intentional, logical, restrictive, organized expansion of a firm. It is calculated and monitored through regular checks and balances or reviews by you or management. The Man-hour Status Spreadsheet is one way to measure controlled growth.

Explosive growth is the unplanned, unintentional, illogical, unrestrictive, unorganized expansion of a firm. It is reactive rather than proactive. It can be intoxicating as well as deadly. Explosive growth vaporizes cash! How many war stories do you know about firms that experienced explosive growth, but crashed and burned due to lack of cash or poor business administration skills, or, worse yet, produced a negligent design due to their lack of experience and were victims of a major lawsuit? Explosive growth will require much of your attention away from the design tasks of the firm. You will need additional staff or outsourced staffing to address the many needs that will arise when you say yes to a large project commitment. In this case, if you are unsure of your business administration skills, it is healthy to think like a designer, and "plan" the staff and schedule growth commitment up front before you sign the contract. Use the Man-hour Status Spreadsheet to measure your projected staffing needs. Close your eyes and envision the future. Use your imagination. The design planning process works very well in the business planning.

To be successful in the long run, you must think of your firm as an oak tree rather than a poplar. A poplar tree grows rapidly and is beautiful, but with a shallow root structure, it can easily be destroyed by a bad windstorm. An oak tree is slow-growing and deep-rooted (the foundation is solid), and it will survive most any storm, even an occasional lightning strike!

A growth plan is the development of the firm's master plan for its future growth and direction. The business plan outlines organization and tactics, the marketing plan outlines vision and strategies, and the growth plan outlines objectives such as these:

Specific targets for branch offices, number of employees, and equipment
Schedules associated with growth
Future needs for capital

Planned growth can be internal or external, or even a combination of both. Internal growth is developed with new equipment, new marketing materials, new spatial requirements, and new images for the firm. External growth develops through mergers and acquisitions, going public, or franchising the operations.

Growth, both internal and external, is a challenging issue to deal with. It can be exciting as well as demoralizing. However, remember that the challenges change daily and make the business world unpredictable. If all of us had the answers, how boring life would be. Plan for growth—and experience a whole new variety of challenges that will make your life more exciting in the future!

Maturity Stage

Every firm is different and reaches the third stage of business life—maturity—in a different time frame. In the maturity stage, the firm reaches its limit in size and performance. By now, the founder of the firm is older, more mature, and not as energetic and enthusiastic about the vitality and excitement of the firm's future. The founder is in a different phase of life: the kids have grown up, personal interests have changed, and the mind and body may not be as quick as they once were.

Experience and poise are the chief characteristics of the founder during this phase of the business. Growth becomes less important. Stability and experience begin to become more important than passion and living on the edge. However, these attributes may not be attractive to all potential clients. If growth is not maintained or rejuvenated by younger staff members, stagnation settles in, and it is only a matter of time before the firm begins to decline. Many designers cannot face the idea of others taking the reigns of the firm that they created. Some may sabotage the firm's future by stopping its growth and eventually closing its doors. If you are your firm's founder, at this stage in the game, you need to maintain a positive perspective on the firm's future. What is your legacy? How do you want you and your firm to be remembered? Will it be "lights out" one day, or will there be a continuation? If you truly believe that we are here on this earth with a mission to help others, then you have a responsibility to turn over the business to the next generation to continue the cause. Professional and financial considerations come into play, but the firm's reputation and tradition of assistance should continue. Should you embrace the change necessary to continue, your firm may re-enter the second phase of business again, but what a difference this time: continuing and refining versus creating. Many second-generation firms have succeeded in this phase of development. Historically, the third generation of a continuum is the most challenging.

Should you decide that you are not interested in revitalizing and continuing the business, ultimately your firm will enter the fourth and final stage of its life.

Decline Stage

Ceasing to grow or refusing to change leads to decay and decline in the fourth stage of the business life cycle. The eventual result is the demise of the firm. But this need not always be the case.

A good example of decline stage "reversal" is Arm & Hammer baking soda. For years, the product was used for baking and cleaning, and as a toothpaste. Eventually, technical and marketing advancements in competitive products made baking soda lose market share. It was about to become extinct when some clever person decided that its odor-absorbing ability made it a wonderful refrigerator deodorant. Whoosh, baking soda roared back to become a stable household item in millions of refrigerators throughout the United States and the world!

Business needs to be flexible, to embrace change and develop fresh new ideas. Leadership is the most important component during this phase of a firm's life. If the decision makers are selfish, and cannot stand the idea of the potential future principals being more successful than they, shame on them, the firm will flounder. Good staff will become de-motivated and leave. Some clientele may leave the firm to work with the younger, less expensive professionals. In this phase of the firm's life, the founding principals need to lead as mentors/parents for the younger professional staff. If they are not aware or cannot behave that way, the firm will stagnate, decline, and die.

MONITORING YOUR PROGRESS
Your New Firm's Vital Signs

Once you establish your goals and deal with your own way of managing fear, risk, guilt, and success, you must act much like a physician and monitor your new firm's vital signs steadily in order to keep it "alive."

The vital signs of the firm are its conscience. These signs raise questions in all areas of the firm, including administration, finance, marketing, and production.

Administration

How can I improve the firm with every situation that I encounter?
How can I be more productive?
Are there any new technologies I can implement that will make us more effective, productive, or profitable?

Finance

How much money does it take to keep the doors open to this office every day?
How much money was received today? Did I receive 1/20 of my monthly need today?
What accounts receivable need attention today?
Did the invoices go out on the tenth of the month?
CASH FLOW! CASH FLOW! CASH FLOW!

What is the ratio of the total of Accounts Receivable + Cash in Hand/ Accounts Payable?

(A great ratio is 2.0/1.0. Making a 3.0/1.0 is amazing. [Your accountant and banker will love this one!] If you are below 1.0/1.0, your firm will be experiencing financial/overhead challenges. If not monitored daily, you will be losing money fast and, before you know it, be "in the red." Operating a business in this financial predicament

can be like living a lie. Be truthful with yourself. If you get in this place of less than 1.0/1.0, you need to cut overhead—mainly staff since they normally equate 80 percent of the firm's overhead.)

Marketing

Did I make two cold calls today?

With whom can I network today, now?

Who do I call to schedule at least two networking lunches a month?

How do I monitor my "just for lunch/network" list?

Do I need to follow up on any proposals?

How does the future workload look compared with the current workload?

What other market opportunities can I investigate?

Production

Am I billable forty hours per week?

Am I managing and delegating my projects in the most effective way?

Which tasks should I do myself; which should I delegate?

Am I understaffed?

Am I making my deadlines?

Am I happy with the firm's production tools?

Am I happy with the quality control on the firm's production work?

Not only must you learn to recognize the vital signs of these four areas:

Administration

Finance

Marketing

Production

but you must also become aware of when to micromanage and macromanage them. You must train yourself to address each sign every day. If you pay too much attention to one, another will suffer. Once again, a critical balance must be maintained on a daily basis.

After twenty-five years' experience, I would say the most important vital sign to monitor every day when the mail arrives is cash received. If you measure how much it costs to operate your firm every month, and divide that figure by twenty business days, you will get an average dollar-per-day figure needed to operate. An example would be that if your firm overhead costs $20,000 per month, then you need at least $1,000 per day during that month to "break-even" with your overhead, not to be confused with your profit. If one day a $3,000 check comes in the mail, your vital sign would be that you are okay for two to three days. If no money comes in for seven working days after that, you are seven days behind making your overhead expenses. This is a great barometer to watch like a hawk. Staying ahead on this vital sign allows you to perform all of the other services you provide. Without cash, there is no company. Remember, cash is king—not design—in a business.

Besides monitoring your firm's vital signs internally, you can obtain outside assistance in evaluating the company and its progress through peer review, business owner support groups, and a mentor.

Peer Review

A peer review is having one or more successful practitioners, preferably not in your market area, evaluate the firm in administration, marketing, production, and finance. The review can help you keep track of your business cycle and progress. Learn from others.

The peer review team seeks to raise the level of a firm's professional practice by determining its objectives, policies, and procedures, and then examining its compliance with the objectives and procedures. The policies and technical competence of the firm are not evaluated by the peer reviewers.

To understand the policies, objectives, and procedures of a firm, the peer review team reviews the written documents furnished by the firm, ahead of time, probing into the following areas:

Management
Development and maintenance of technical competence
Management of projects
Human resources
Financial management
Business development

For smaller firms, the peer reviewers will interview the principal and key personnel if the firm's objectives and procedures are mentally established but not recorded.

The peer review is systematic and depends on communication and coordination. Its procedures, established and monitored by the American Consulting Engineers Council (ACEC), are as follows:

Firm requests peer review from ACEC.
Firm selects peer reviewers from list provided by ACEC.
ACEC coordinates schedules of reviewers and firm and establishes
    date of review.
ACEC gives list of materials required by firm to forward to reviewers.
Reviewers forward agreement of nondisclosure to firm.
Peer review is conducted.
Peer reviewers give verbal report at end of review to CEO.
Firm critiques the peer review and work of the reviewers.

The cost of the peer review is small compared with the benefit and value a firm will receive from having it. The firm pays for the travel and lodging expenses incurred by the review team along with an administrative fee and honoraria for the reviewers. Member firms of the ACEC and AIA pay a little less than nonmembers. The scale of the review is based on the size of the firm. In general, the following rules of thumb apply:

Firms with 1–15 staff	2 reviewers/1 day
Firms with 16–25 staff	2 reviewers/2 days
Firms with 26–60 staff	3 reviewers/2 days
Firms with more than 60 staff	3 or 4 reviewers/2 days

The problem many design firm principals have with a peer review is that they cannot bring themselves to open the firm and its management to criticism. As designers, we have been trained to accept constructive criticism on design, and we can review our employees' job performance according to our own criteria. However, having our abilities criticized as to how we run our firm—no way! It is important not to let yourself become defensive. How can we become more effective unless we learn from others? None of us is perfect, especially in running a business!

A peer review gives you a snapshot of how your firm is doing. Check with your liability insurance carrier. Some carriers will reimburse you for the expense of conducting a peer review because they recognize that you are trying to learn from the past and improve your practice, thus diminishing the risk of future liability claims.

A formal peer review should be a goal to achieve in the future. A review is generally not necessary for a young firm during the first few years. However, simply discussing the challenges and issues that you face day-to-day with colleagues and mentors is, to a degree, a minor peer review. Don't be afraid to share your concerns with friends and other colleagues. Designers often join the AIA in order to meet other practitioners who face the same issues. Many chapters have "small firm roundtables" and sole-proprietor groups.

Business Owner Support Groups

Business owner support groups provide another source of psychological help for coping with the current stage of your firm's business cycle. These groups are comprised of six to ten individuals who meet once a month to discuss matters that affect their respective businesses.

For many, this is the way to go because the program is structured so that no two business owners who would be considered competitors are assigned to the same group. Another benefit is that all members of the group are total strangers. For many, this is the ultimate go-ahead to allow themselves to share their fears and secrets with others. For others, it takes a few sessions before trust and bonding develop so they can open up to the group.

Interestingly, no matter what line of work or profession you are in, the same business problems and issues arise. You may hear about someone else's problem and think that it cannot possibly affect your firm, but you never know. Also, having the opportunity to help others solve their business problems deepens your character and experience, and will help you deal more effectively with your own business problems.

Business owner support groups usually meet for a two-and-a-half-hour session, divided into three forty-five-minute segments. The first segment begins with the facilitator opening up the floor to discussion on business events that occurred in the past thirty days. Each participant summarizes, in fifty words or less, the trends and unique events that he or she has encountered. It is amazing how similar the reported issues are. The next segment is a "roundtable" in which one, two, or three issues are discussed by all. The final segment is usually focused on the vision quest of one business owner.

The owner presents his or her background, the history of the company, its market and organization, and his or her vision of where the company is heading. The owner describes the problems he or she feels the firm will encounter as well as the firm's strengths and weaknesses. The group asks questions and critiques the presenter's information. Guidance is provided on many issues that the owner might have a difficult time discussing with a spouse, partner, or friend. Business is business, and owners understand owners.

Joining a group like this provides valuable feedback as well as a potential network of opportunities! Contact your local chamber of commerce to see if a business owner support group has been established in your area.

Mentors

A mentor is a trusted counselor or guide.

Since the beginning of the business enterprise, more experienced individuals have provided advice to newer/younger individuals in the business. Some mentors are senior partners in the same firm, others are outside the design firm, or maybe in another business. It is always beneficial to have an elder, more experienced individual as a consulter to help you address your inexperience, address fears of the known and unknown, and draw comfort out of their knowledge base. Mentors can be a calming influence on your performance and success. When and if you start your firm by yourself, you will find it at times a very lonely experience. Having a mentor can help guide you through many of those challenges. Having a mentor is having a special relationship with someone who really knows you and cares about your success. To have one is to be very fortunate in life.

EVERY DAY IS DIFFERENT

The future of your firm is here, today, now. The fact is that no matter how experienced you are or how old your firm is, like every other business owner, you must restart every day! As with an automobile, you turn over the engine with the ignition and starter every single morning.

Every new day brings fresh new challenges to face, requiring new solutions. These solutions may be based upon former ones (experience) or on advice from others. However, one thing is clear: No matter how mundane or repetitive things seem on the surface, every day is different. This is what is so

exiting about operating your own firm. It never gets dull. It may get fatigu-
ing, but it is never boring.

So if you are considering starting your own firm, what are you waiting
for? Join the rest of us in the business arena who launch new firms every day!
Learn to depend on your friends, your significant other, and your colleagues.
Make this book your silent partner. Write in it, share its ideas, carry it with
you, keep it in a very accessible place.

This book comes with no guarantees. However, if you follow the suggestions made throughout its chapters, you stand a good chance of achieving success. Remember these rules of thumb:

Be honest, forthright, and genuine.
Make others feel important.
Grow your contact network.
Market yourself to everyone and everything.
Learn to negotiate.
Learn how to sell yourself.
Subcontract with other designers to improve your profits.
Follow up on all marketing leads.
Rely on and trust your accountant, attorney, and bookkeeper.
Monitor your firm's vital signs, *especially cash flow in every day's mail.*
Maintain the necessary critical balance in your life.
Approach your business fresh and with confidence.
Take time out to charge up your batteries.
Don't give up! You must not lose sight of your goal.
Maintain a sense of humor.
Learn to take risks.
Learn to manage fear, guilt, and success.

Remember to share your good experiences with your friends, colleagues,
and significant other or family, because you will certainly be sharing the bad
ones with them during your journey! Be considerate of them, because life
without them would be impossible.

Set obtainable goals. Maintain your vision for your company, and above all
be flexible in your practice. Learn to accept the bad events that you will
inevitably encounter. In business as well as life, no one can fully appreciate the
good without understanding and appreciating the bad.

Learn to accept that you will receive all the business that you need, not necessarily all the business that you want.

Learn from your mistakes as well as those of others. Take manageable risks, and exercise your business conscience in every single matter that you handle. Stay focused, passionate, and aggressive. Manage your fear, your clients, your partner(s), your employees, and most important, yourself!

Set a good example for others by utilizing a selfless leadership style in your everyday activity. Your admirable behavior may inspire them to do their job better.

One final note of hope is that when you are successful, living well will be the best revenge. Good luck and . . .

Make it happen!!!!!!!!!!!!!!

Recommended Readings

Act Like an Owner: Building an Ownership Culture, by Robert Blonchek and Martin O'Neill. Published by John Wiley and Sons, Inc., 1999.

First Things First, by Stephen R. Covey, A. Roger Merrill, and Rebecca R. Merrill. Published by Simon & Schuster, 1994.

Good to Great, by Jim Collins. Published by Harper Business, New York, 2001.

Leadership Jazz, by Max DePree. Published by Dell Publishing, 1992.

Leadership Is an Art, by Max DePree. Published by Dell Publishing, 1989.

Pour Your Heart Into It: How Starbucks Built a Company One Cup at a Time, by Howard Schultz and Dori Jones Yang. Published by Hyperion, New York, 1997.

The E Myth Revisited, by Michael E. Gerber. Published by Harper Business, New York, 1995.

Appendix A: Sample Design Proposal

June 1, 2007

Mr. & Mrs. Robert L. Smith
601 Crest Horn Road
Towson, Maryland 00000

Re: Residential addition to 601 Crest Horn Road

Dear Mr. and Mrs. Smith:

Apple Architecture, Inc., is pleased to present this proposal for professional architectural services to design and produce construction documents for the proposed great room/kitchen/bedroom addition to 601 Crest Horn Road in Towson.

SCOPE OF WORK

As discussed in our first meeting on Tuesday, May 26, 2007, it is our understanding that you plan to construct a new great room/kitchen/bedroom addition (approximately 900 square feet, on two levels) on the south side of your home.

Your hope is to connect the addition to the existing house across the entire 33-foot length of the south elevation and enclose the existing breezeway, which connects to the existing garage. Further, you desire to renovate/"modernize" the existing kitchen, upgrading the cabinetry, countertops, and appliances. Your plan is to construct the addition of wood frame with a crawl space in lieu of a basement. The exterior finish can be brick or siding, which will depend solely on the budget.

The great room is to "bring the outdoors inside," with the use of as much glass as possible to provide a view of the existing backyard. It is to be open to the existing living room and it is to have bookshelves but no fireplace. There is a desire to have a vaulted (cathedral) ceiling in the space.

The kitchen addition is to provide space for a dining table for four to six. It, like the great room, is to have a view of the backyard. The kitchen modernization is to include new appliances, cabinetry, and countertops, and is to be connected to the new eating area.

The new master bedroom is to be located on the addition's second floor. It is to have its own private bathroom, including water closet, double-bowl vanity, and tub/shower unit (or, if possible, a tub with separate shower). The bedroom is to be seventeen (17) feet by seventeen (17) feet minimum, in size. Sixteen (16) to twenty (20) lineal feet of closet space is to be provided. A secondary "back" stair is to be studied for inclusion in the project, providing access to the area from the first level.

The new addition is to have its own HVAC system zone. Since the existing house has gas-fired heat only, it appears that a gas-fired heating and air conditioning system for the new addition is logical. Further, the goal for the project is to add a new air conditioning unit to the existing house HVAC system, utilizing the existing forced-air ductwork.

Finally, an outdoor wood deck is to be master planned off the rear of the house. At this time, the deck may be considered an alternate. (We will design, but not produce, construction documents for a building permit.)

Your hope is to build the two-storey addition and kitchen alteration for approximately $300,000.00 (900 square feet at $333.00 per square foot plus $50,000 for the kitchen upgrade). This figure does not include contingency fees, or furnishings.

Finally, we discussed a scope of work necessary to accomplish your project.

We have organized our services to accomplish the scope of work into the following five phases:

Phase I. Field Measurement and Documentation of Existing Conditions
Phase II. Conceptual Design
Phase III. Construction Document
Phase IV. Bid (optional)
Phase V. Construction Administration (optional)

Phase I. Field Measurement and Documentation of Existing Conditions

Upon receipt of an approved, executed proposal, we will schedule a mutually agreeable time to visit your home and field measure the first floor, second floor, and basement. Further, we will photograph the interior as well as the exterior of the house to document the existing conditions. We estimate that we will need approximately one-half day to conduct this exercise.

After completion of our field survey, we will return to our office and draft the existing first floor, second floor, and basement floor plans. Additionally, we will draft the existing south (rear) and east and west (side) elevations. Upon completion, we will forward one copy of the drawings to you for your review.

Time frame: 1 week
Fee: $4,500 on an hourly, not-to-exceed basis

Phase II. Conceptual Design

Apple Architecture, Inc., will develop alternate conceptual floor plan designs based upon the scope of the project. Our documentation will include floor plans and a site plan for your review at one meeting in our office. The goal of our review meeting will be to refine the many ideas presented into one approved design. This approved concept will be refined into a final site plan, floor plan, and elevations to be presented at a final design review meeting in our office. The approved design will be presented to one or two contractors at a future meeting to confirm the conceptual budget for the addition.

Time frame: 4 weeks
Fee: $9,500.00 on an hourly, not-to-exceed basis

Phase III. Construction Document

Upon approval of the conceptual design phase and conceptual design budget, we will proceed with the construction document phase, producing construction drawings and specifications for building permit applications and for the basis of construction.

At this time, we have figured an allowance of time (60 to 80 hours) to produce the necessary construction documents. We felt that quoting the range was the most fair to you and our firm. We shall endeavor to conduct our services within this range of time.

Time frame: 8 weeks
Fee: $19,500.00 on an hourly, not-to-exceed basis

Phase IV. Bid (Optional)

Upon completion of the construction document phase, we can assist you on the coordination of pricing for the addition and answer any questions that the contractors may have concerning the design and drawings. Services could be for a one-time exercise with up to five (5) bidders.

Time frame: 3 weeks
Fee: $2,500.00 on an hourly, not-to-exceed basis

Phase V. Construction Administration (Optional)

We estimate that your addition will have a construction time frame of approximately 4 to 6 months. Experience tells us that we may average approximately 2 hours per week during that 16- to 26-week period, answering questions, making eight site visits, developing one punch list walk-through, one final walk-through, and reviewing submittals for your project. Therefore, we recommend a time allowance in which we will bill you by the hour, not to exceed 50 hours on construction administration time for our architectural staff.

Time frame: 16 to 26 weeks
Fee: $12,500.00 on an hourly, not-to-exceed basis

Summary of Fees

Phase I. Document existing conditions	$4,500.00
Phase II. Conceptual design	$9,500.00
Phase III. Construction documents	$19,500.00
Subtotal	$33,500.00
(On an hourly, not-to-exceed basis)	

Optional Services
Phase IV. Bid/negotiation $2,500.00
Phase V. Construction administration $12,500.00
(On an hourly, not-to-exceed basis)

Exclusions

Please note that the above quoted figures do not include any of the following:

Professional land survey
Civil engineering design
Mechanical, electrical, plumbing engineering design
Landscape architecture design (conceptual patio design is included
  in the proposal)
Structural engineering of special conditions or retaining-wall design
Cost estimating
Kitchen design
Appliance selection
Special stereo and security system selection
Furniture inventory and selection
Accessory and artwork selection
Interior design services
Permit filing or expediting fees with Baltimore County

Reimbursable Expenses

Reimbursable expenses such as printing, photography, long distance communications, and application and filing of a building permit, soil borings, etc., will be
provided on an as-needed basis and will be billed monthly with a 15 percent
administrative charge.

Additional Services

Should additional services be requested by you due to a change in scope of the
services required, we will proceed with the said services upon your written
approval, and invoice on an hourly basis based on the following hourly rates:

Principal $150.00
Managing architect $95.00

Staff architect	$75.00
Staff designer	$55.00
Administrative	$40.00
Managing interior designer	$75.00

Miscellaneous Provisions

Invoices will be sent monthly, with payment due within 30 days of receipt. Should the production effort be interrupted due to late receipt of payments, it will be necessary to adjust the schedule. Interest will be billed at the rate of 1.5 percent per month on the balance outstanding, 30 days after the date of the invoice, and will be added and compounded monthly.

We specifically reserve the right to suspend or terminate our services if payment is not received within the time period specified.

We reserve the right to withhold plans and documents from the review, signature, or distribution process, if account is not currently paid.

This proposal will remain in effect for a period of not less than one year from the effective date hereof. At that time, we reserve the right to revise our rates in accordance with changes in our operating costs. Written notification will be given 30 days prior to the effective date of any such change in rates.

Please advise as soon as possible as to the status of our proposal so that we may schedule our work accordingly.

If this proposal is satisfactory, please sign where indicated and return the enclosed copy as your acceptance of its terms and as our authorization to proceed.

As always, should you have any questions concerning any of the above information, please feel free to contact me. It was a pleasure meeting with you to discuss various issues relating to your needs. We look forward to working with you on your challenging project.

Regards,
George Macintosh Apple III, AIA
President
Apple Architecture, Inc.

Acceptance

The proposed description of professional services and terms are satisfactory and are hereby accepted. Authorization to proceed with the work is granted.

The terms of this proposal shall be null and void if not accepted within 60 days.

Name _____

Date _____

Appendix B: Glossary of Accounting Terms

Accounting: The recording and reporting of all business transactions for use in making future business decisions.

Accounting Cycle: Source documents, journal, ledger, trial balance, adjustments (accruals), adjusted trial balance, income statement, balance sheet, closing entries, and postclosing trial balance.

Accounting Equation: Assets = liabilities + owner's equity.

Accounting Period: The length of time for which an income statement is customarily prepared.

Accounts Payable: An amount (liability) owed to a creditor (consultant, blueprinter, vendor, etc.), generally on an open account.

Accounts Receivable: A claim (asset) against a debtor (client) for services performed.

Accrual Basis: The practice of recording a revenue or expense transaction (accounts receivable or accounts payable) during the accounting period in which it occurs rather than in the period when actual payment is made or recognized.

Asset: Anything of monetary (cash) value owned by a business (furniture, equipment, etc.).

Audit: Any inspection by a third person of accounting records involving analysis, testing, proof, and confirmation.

Balance Sheet: A statement showing the status of all assets, liabilities, and owner's equity on a specific date.

Book Value: The value of a stock determined from a company's records by adding all assets (excluding goodwill) and then deducting all debts and other liabilities plus the liquidation price of any preferred issues. The sum arrived at is divided by the number of common shares outstanding and the result is book value per common share.

Bookkeeping: The recording of financial data from source documents to journals and ledgers.

Capital: The owner's investment in a business; not synonymous with cash. Capital can include cash, equipment, furniture, or any asset.

Cash: Money (currency and coins), money orders, bank deposits, and bank credit card balances; the first asset listed on the balance sheet.

Cash Basis: The practice of recording income and expenses only when cash is actually received or paid out.

Cash Discount: The amount, usually a percentage (%), that a vendor will deduct from the total price for prompt payment.

Creditor: An entity that loans or gives credit in a business transaction.

Depreciation: The monetary loss in service, capacity, or utility from a fixed asset (car, computer, furniture, etc.); a type of business expense.

Expense: A cost of operating a business (telephone, salaries, rent, letterhead, business cards, etc.); also called overhead.

General Ledger: The book of original bookkeeping entries, in which data from source documents is first recorded.

Gross Margin: Total fees minus the cost of services sold; also called markup.

Income Statement: A statement providing information about revenue and expenses over a specific period of time.

Liability: An obligation of a business to pay a debt (account payable, note payable, etc.) to a creditor.

Liquidity: The ability of a business to readily convert all accounts receivable and other assets into cash.

Note: An unconditional written promise to pay a certain sum of money.

Owner's Equity: The net worth of the business, defined as capital + income − expenses.

Payroll: A record showing the wages and salaries earned by employees along with various deductions (for withholding taxes, insurance, retirement plans, etc.).

Petty Cash: A small amount of cash on hand, used for minor disbursements, when payment by check is impractical.

Posting: The process of recording information from a journal to the general ledger.

Prepaid Expenses: Current assets that become expenses as they are used; supplies are an example.

Retained Earnings: An accumulation of earnings which have not been paid out to stockholders in a corporation.

Return on Investment: The ratio of profits to net worth or stockholders' equity.

Revenue: Any source of income for a business.

Transaction: Any business activity involving an exchange of money values.

Trial Balance: A list of all accounts proving the ledger; debits must equal credits.

Appendix C: Glossary of Legal Terms

Affidavit: A sworn statement in writing.

Affirmative Action: A court-ordered requirement that employers who, in the court's judgment, have practiced job discrimination against a minority in the past extend favorable treatment to minority members in the work force.

Annual Percentage Rate (APR): The true interest rate, arrived at by taking into consideration all finance charges.

Arbitration: The hearing and determination of a civil dispute by a person or persons chosen or approved by both parties.

Capital Stock: The total stock issued by a corporation.

Chapter 7: A section of the Federal Bankruptcy Act which grants debtors the right to clear themselves of debt by paying a percentage or nothing of what they owe.

Chapter 13: A section of the Federal Bankruptcy Act which grants debtors the right to pay off all or part of their debts on an easy payment plan under protection of the court.

Contract: An agreement upon sufficient consideration to do or not to do a particular act.

Corporation: A form of business regarded by law as a person, distinct from the persons who own it; owners are therefore not responsible for the debts of the corporation.

Defendant: The person against whom a legal action is brought.

General Partnership: A partnership in which each member is responsible for the acts of the other partners and for all partnership debts.

Goodwill: An intangible asset arising from the reputation of a business and its relations with its customers; distinct from the value of business stock and other tangible assets.

Lien: A legal claim against property, usually as a result of debt.

Limited Partnership: A partnership in which the liability of some of the members (limited partners) is restricted to the amount of their respective investments.

Litigation: A method of resolving disputes through a legal contest carried out by judicial process.

Mediation: A method of intervening in a civil dispute to promote reconciliation, compromise, or settlement; solutions may or may not be accepted by the contending parties.

Negligence: Failure to exercise reasonable care, resulting in accidental injury to another person or persons.

Partnership: An agreement of two or more parties to conduct an unincorporated business.

Plaintiff: A person who brings a lawsuit or civil action to a court; the complaining person.

Preferred Stock: Stock that is superior to common stock with respect to dividends and often to asset sharing in the event of liquidation.

Sole Proprietorship: An unincorporated business with a single owner.

Statute: A law enacted by a legislature and expressed in a formal document.

Statutory Law: A body of law enacted by a legislature.

Stock: The ownership shares of a corporation authorized by its articles of incorporation, including both common and preferred stock.

Stockholder: A holder or owner of stock in a corporation.

Tort: A wrongful act resulting in damage or injury, often willfully or negligently performed, for which a civil suit can be brought.

Appendix D: Glossary of Banking Terms

Amortization: The gradual reduction of debt by means of equal periodic payments sufficient to meet current interest and liquidate the debt at maturity.

Appreciation: The increase in value of an asset in excess of its depreciable cost as a result of economic and other conditions; distinguished from increases in value arising from improvements or additions to the asset.

Average Daily Balance: The average amount of money that a customer keeps on deposit, determined by adding the daily balances of an account for a given length of time and dividing the total by the number of days.

Bad Debts: Amounts due on open accounts receivable that have proved uncollectible.

Bank Reconciliation: Verification of a bank statement balance and the depositor's checkbook balance.

Depreciation: The amount of expense charged against business earnings in order to write off the cost of a plant or machine over its useful life, giving consideration to wear and tear, obsolescence, and salvage. Under straight-line depreciation, the expense is assumed to be incurred in equal amounts in each business year over the life of the asset. Under accelerated depredation, the expense is assumed to be incurred in decreasing amounts in each business year over the life of the asset.

Line of Credit: An agreement between a bank and a company whereby the bank lends the company funds up to a previously agreed upon maximum amount. A line of credit is used by business for future commitments and purchases in times of growth or slow cash flow.

Liquidity: The solvency of a business, or the degree to which its assets can readily be converted into cash without loss.

Long-Term Debt: An obligation that will not become due for at least one year.

Mortgage: A written obligation to pay a debt over time, with the underlying asset pledged as security.

Nonforfeiture Option: One of the choices available if the policyholder discontinues premium payments on a policy with a cash value. It may be taken in liquid cash, or as extended term insurance, or as reduced, paid-up insurance.

Retained Earnings: An accumulation of earnings which have not been paid out to stockholders.

Secured Loan: A loan that is secured by marketable securities or other marketable valuables.

Short-Term Debt: An obligation which will be due in full within a one-year time frame.

Term Loan: A long-term loan with a life of up to ten years.

Unsecured Loan: A loan that is not secured by a marketable security or asset.

Appendix E: Glossary of Insurance Terms

Accumulation Period: A specified length of time during which the insured must incur eligible medical expenses at least equal to the deductible amount to establish a benefit period under a medical policy.

Actuary: A trained professional in the technical aspects of insurance mathematics (calculations of premiums, reserves, annuities, and other values).

Adjustable Life Insurance: An insurance plan that allows the policyholder to change certain terms: raise or lower the face value of the policy, increase or decrease the premium, and lengthen or shorten the protection period.

Age Limits: Established minimum and maximum ages for which an insurance company will not accept applications or renew policies.

Agent: An insurance company representative licensed by the state who solicits and sells insurance and services claims made by policyholders.

Aggregate Indemnity: The maximum dollar amount that may be collected for any disability or period of disability under an insurance policy.

Allocated Benefits: Benefits for which the maximum amount payable for specific services is itemized in the contract.

Beneficiary: The person designated or provided for by the policy terms to receive the benefits of the policy.

Benefits: The amount paid by the insurance company to a claimant or beneficiary under coverage.

Broker: An insurance solicitor licensed by a state who places business with a variety of insurance companies.

Business Insurance: An insurance policy that provides coverage of benefits to a business rather than an individual. It is issued to indemnify a business for loss or services when a key employee or a partner becomes disabled.

Business Life Insurance: Insurance purchased by a business on the life of a member of the firm. It is purchased to protect the surviving owners or partners from loss of services when a key employee or partner dies.

Cash Surrender Value: The amount available in cash upon voluntary termination of a policy by its owner, before the policy becomes payable by death or maturity.

Certificate of Insurance: A statement of coverage issued to an individual insured under a group insurance contract, outlining the insurance benefits and principal provisions applicable to the member.

Claim: Notification to an insurance company that payment of an amount is being sought under the terms of a particular policy.

Convertible Term Insurance: Term insurance that can be exchanged, at the policyholder's option and without evidence of insurability, for another plan of insurance.

Credit Life Insurance: Term life insurance issued through a lender to cover payment of a loan in the case of death.

Deductible: The amount of covered charges that must be paid by the policyholder before benefits can be realized from the insurance company.

Deposit Term Insurance: A form of term insurance in which the first-year premium is larger than subsequent premiums.

Disability: A partial or total physical or mental handicap resulting from sickness or injury.

Disability Benefit: A policy feature providing for the waiver of a premium, and sometimes payment of monthly income, if the policyholder becomes totally and permanently disabled.

Disability Income Insurance: A form of insurance that provides payments to replace income when the policyholder becomes disabled as a result of illness or injury.

Dividend: A return on part of a premium to a policyholder that reflects the difference between the actual premium charged and a combination of the insurance company's actual mortality, expense, and investment experience.

Double Indemnity: A policy provision that doubles payment of a designated benefit when certain kinds of fatal accidents occur.

Duplication of Benefits: The overlapping or identical coverage of the same policyholder under two or more health plans.

Effective Date: The date on which coverage under an insurance policy begins.

Eligibility Date: The date on which an individual or a particular group becomes eligible to apply for insurance under a group life or health insurance plan.

Eligibility Period: A specified length of time following the eligibility date during which an individual or a particular group will remain eligible to apply for insurance under a group life or health insurance policy without evidence of insurability.

Eligible Employees: Members of a group who have met the eligibility requirements under a group life or health plan.

Elimination Period: A period of time between the period of disability and the start of disability income insurance benefits, during which no benefits are payable.

Evidence of Insurability: Any statement of proof of a person's physical condition and/or other factual information affecting the individual's eligibility for insurance.

Exclusions: Specific conditions or circumstances listed in the policy for which no benefit payments will be provided.

Extended Term Insurance: A form of insurance, available as a nonforfeiture option, in which the original amount of insurance is provided for a limited period of time.

Grace Period: A period following the premium date during which an overdue premium may be paid without penalty.

Group Life Insurance: Life insurance provided to a group of people under a master policy.

Health Insurance: Insurance protection that provides payment of benefits for covered sickness or injury.

Health Maintenance Organization (HMO): An organization that provides a wide range of healthcare services for a specified group at a fixed periodic payment.

Hospital Expense Insurance: Protection against the cost of hospital care resulting from the illness or injury of the policyholder.

Insurance: Protection by written contract (policy) against hazards.

Key Person Health Insurance: An individual or group insurance policy designed to protect a business against loss of income resulting from the disability of a key employee.

Level Premium: A premium that remains unchanged throughout the life of a policy.

Level Premium Life Insurance: A life insurance policy in which the premium remains the same from year to year.

Lifetime Disability Benefit: A benefit to help replace income lost by a policyholder for as long as he or she is totally disabled—even for a lifetime.

Long-Term Disability Income Insurance: Insurance issued to an employer group or individual to provide for replacement of a portion of an employee's earned income lost as a result of serious and prolonged illness or injury.

Major Medical Insurance: Health insurance to cover the expenses of major illness and injury.

Ordinary Life Insurance: Life insurance issued in amounts of $1,000 or more, with premiums payable on an annual, semiannual, quarterly, or monthly basis.

Overhead Insurance: A type of short-term disability income insurance that reimburses the insured person for specified, fixed monthly expenses that are normal and customary in the operation of a business.

Paid-up Insurance: Insurance on which all required premiums have been paid.

Permanent Life Insurance: Insurance that accrues in cash value, such as whole life insurance or an endowment.

Policy Loan: A loan made by the insurance company to the policyholder on the security of the cash value of the policy.

Policyholder: The person, partnership, or corporation that owns the insurance policy.

Premium: The payment that the policyholder agrees to make to keep an insurance policy in force.

Preexisting Condition: A physical and/or mental condition of an insured policyholder that first manifested itself prior to issuance of the policy or that existed and was given treatment prior to issuance.

Preferred Provider Organization (PPO): A group of medical-care providers that furnish services to a group at lower than usual fees in exchange for an agreement guaranteeing prompt payment and a certain volume of patients.

Renewal: Continuation of coverage beyond the original agreement by the policyholder's acceptance of the premium for a new policy term.

Renewable Term Insurance: Term insurance that can be renewed at the end of a term at the option of the policyholder.

Rider: A special policy provision or group of provisions added to a policy to expand or limit the benefits otherwise payable.

Self-Insurance: A program for providing group insurance with benefits financed entirely by the employer in place of purchasing coverage from commercial insurance companies.

Short-Term Disability Income Insurance: Insurance that pays benefits to a disabled policyholder for a specified period of time, usually not exceeding two years.

Straight Life Insurance: Whole life insurance in which premiums are payable for the life of the policyholder.

Term Insurance: Life insurance that has no cash value unless the policyholder dies within a specified time period; benefits are payable only to the beneficiary.

Third-Party Administrator: A business that administrates group health insurance plans for associations and dubs.

Universal Life Insurance: A flexible-premium life insurance policy under which the policyholder may change the death benefit from time to time and vary the amount or timing of premium payments.

Variable Life Insurance: Life insurance under which the benefit relates to the value of assets behind the contract at the time the benefit is paid.

Waiting Period: The length of time an employee must wait to gain insurance coverage from an employer.

Whole Life Insurance: Life insurance that develops a cash value, which may be drawn upon or cashed out by the policyholder (e.g., for retirement purposes) or paid out to a beneficiary at the death of the policyholder.

Workers' Compensation: Insurance to pay benefits and furnish care to employees injured on the job or to compensate dependents of employees killed on the job.

About the Author

Albert W. Rubeling, Jr., FAIA, is the founder and a partner in Rubeling & Associates, Inc., an architectural and interior design firm based outside of Baltimore, in Towson, Maryland. His areas of expertise are in Vision Planning and Master Planning for private educational and religious organizations.

He has been very active on numerous design practice and intern development-related committees of the American Institute of Architects (AIA) over the past twenty years. He has conducted seminars and has lectured on this topic throughout the United States. He also serves as a Trustee for The Boys' Latin School of Maryland and the Community College of Baltimore County's Foundation Board.

A regulator of architectural practice, Mr. Rubeling served two terms on the Maryland State Board of Architects. He is currently a Trustee for the AIA Trust. He has also served as president of the Baltimore and Maryland Chapters of the AIA and, being a past national board member, is a Richard Upjohn Fellow of the AIA.

He obtained his Bachelor of Architecture from the University of Maryland School of Architecture and is licensed to practice architecture in twenty states. He founded the firm in 1981, and "starts it, every morning."

Index

dead end job, 9
depreciation
   accounting for, 59–60
   defined, 60
   methods of, 60
design practice, 5
design proposal, sample
   acceptance, 223
   additional services, 221–222
   bid, 220
   conceptual design, 219
   construction administration, 220
   construction document, 219–220
   exclusions, 221
   field measurement and documentation,
      218–219
   miscellaneous provisions, 222
   reimbursable expenses, 221
   scope, 217–218
   summary of fees, 220–221
design training, 4

employee, advantages, 11
employer, drawbacks, 11
employment, no opportunities at former, 9
entrepreneur
   defined, 12
   imagination of, 6
   personal evaluation of, 13–14
   qualities needed, 12–14
   reasons for starting firm, 12
expenditures
   bookkeeping documentation, 54
   money management of, 42

failure
   to file taxes, 68–70
   perspective of, 11
fear
   attitude and, 170–173
   defined, 170
   management of, 176–179
   real v. imagined, 170–171
   starting firm and, vii, 26–27, 169–170
federal unemployment taxes (FUTA), 65
fees
   establishment of, 46–49
   overhead and, 47–52
   rate structure for, 46–47
FICA. *See* social security payroll taxes
first year
   goals, establishment of, 21
   hours required for, 48
   inspiration from, 3

founder, 196–197
FUTA. *See* federal unemployment
   taxes

glossary terms
   accounting, 225–227
   banking, 231–232
   business/legal, 229–230
   insurance, 233–238
goals
   annual, 33–34
   bad, 31–32
   complexity of, 34
   daily, 32–33
   financial achievement of, 21
   first year, 21
   good, 31
   hope blinded by, 21
   monthly, 33
   number of, 34
   obtaining, 32
   for profit, 50–51, 52
   results and measurement of, 34
   routine in, 32
   weekly, 33
growth
   controlled v. explosive, 204–205
   decision for, 201–204
guilt
   business conscience and, 175–176
   defined, 175
   management of, 176–179

image, 87–89, 90
imagination, 29
   application of, 31
   of entrepreneur, 6
   of partner, 30
   strategies from, 31
income taxes, 63, 65
inspiration, from first year, 3
insurance
   glossary terms for, 233–238
   managing risk and, 135
   need for, 123–125
   obtaining, 126
   practicing without, 133–134
   types of, 126–132
investment
   of accounts receivable, 44
   money, 27
   profits, 47
   for startup capital, 37, 38, 41
   time, 26, 27

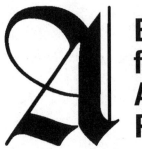

Books from Allworth Press

Allworth Press is an imprint of Allworth Communications, Inc. Selected titles are listed below.

Business and Legal Forms for Interior Designers
by Tad Crawford and Eva Doman Bruck (paperback, with CD-ROM, 8 ½ × 11, 240 pages, $29.95)

The Interior Designer's Guide to Pricing, Estimating, and Budgeting
by Theo Stephan Williams (paperback, 6 × 9, 208 pages, $19.95)

Licensing Art and Design, Revised Edition
by Caryn R. Leland (paperback, 6 × 9, 128 pages, $16.95)

The Real Business of Web Design
by John Waters (paperback, 6 × 9, 256 pages, $19.95)

Creating the Perfect Design Brief: How to Manage Design for Strategic Advantage
by Peter L. Phillips (paperback, 6 × 9, 224 pages, $19.95)

Starting Your Career As a Freelance Illustrator or Graphic Designer, Revised Edition
by Michael Fleishman (paperback, 6 × 9, 272 pages, $19.95)

Inside the Business of Graphic Design: 60 Leaders Share Their Secrets of Success
By Catharine Fishel (paperback, 6 × 9, 288 pages, $19.95)

How to Grow as a Graphic Designer
by Catharine Fishel (paperback, 6 × 9, 256 pages, $19.95)

The Graphic Designer's and Illustrator's Guide to Marketing and Promotion
by Maria Piscopo (paperback, 6 × 9, 224 pages, $19.95)

The Graphic Design Business Book
by Tad Crawford (paperback, 6 × 9, 256 pages, $24.95)

AIGA Professional Practices in Graphic Design: The American Institute of Graphic Arts
edited by Tad Crawford (paperback, 6 ¾ × 9 ⅞, 320 pages, $24.95)

Please write to request our free catalog. To order by credit card, call 1-800-491-2808 or send a check or money order to Allworth Press, 10 East 23rd Street, Suite 510, New York, NY 10010. Include $6 for shipping and handling for the first book ordered and $1 for each additional book. Eleven dollars plus $1 for each additional book if ordering from Canada. New York State residents must add sales tax.

To see our complete catalog on the World Wide Web, or to order online, you can find us at ***www.allworth.com.***